U:

D:

This b
self

CHILDREN
IN THE PUBLIC CARE

Sir William Utting

A REVIEW OF

RESIDENTIAL

CHILD CARE

London: HMSO

CONTENTS

PREFACE

1. I was instructed by the Secretary of State on 28 May 1991

    "to carry out a special review of residential child care in England. I undertook to consider all matters bearing upon residential child care, including the availability of resources of all kinds; to concentrate particularly on arrangements for the monitoring and control of residential child care; to review the programme of action affecting residential care which is being introduced by the Children Act in October; and to report by 31 July, recommending such further action as seemed necessary."

2. The review and its terms of reference were occasioned by public concern about standards and practices in residential child care following publication of "The Pindown Experience and the Protection of Children: the Report of the Staffordshire Child Care Inquiry 1990" (Staffordshire County Council 1991). I was subsequently asked, as a result of further disquieting incidents, to make clear that my remit extended to the care being provided for children in institutions other than children's homes.

3. I have had the assistance of a dedicated group throughout, led for the Department by Edmund Waterhouse and for the Social Services Inspectorate by John Rowlands, supported by Jim Brown (Executive Officer) and Valerie Rowe (Senior Personal Secretary), and further helped by Diana Robbins (Research Consultant). Their ability and commitment have been outstanding. I record my deep gratitude to them, individually and collectively. This has been a testing task; but they have made it an enjoyable one as well.

4. I have also been helped by contributions and comments from other colleagues at the Department of Health. I am especially grateful to those who designed and analysed the survey of staff in twenty local authorities, and to the Directors and officers of those authorities whose speedy turnround of information made the survey possible.

5. I was eager to consult interests independent of Government. A number of people gave generously of their time and greatly helped me in clarifying issues and suggesting remedies; but the views and conclusions I express in this report are my own. A list of witnesses is at Appendix 2. Other individuals and organisations offered written comment. They are listed at Appendix 3.

6. The report that follows is in two parts: the first contains a relatively brief discussion of the issues and lists main recommendations; the second part deals with the issues and arguments in more depth and ends with a chapter of general conclusions and a full list of recommendations.

Sir William Utting

CHILDREN
IN THE PUBLIC CARE

A REVIEW OF

RESIDENTIAL

CHILD CARE

PART 1

INTRODUCTION

BACKGROUND

1. This review was commissioned by the Secretary of State following the publication of the 'Pindown Experience' Report (Staffordshire County Council 1991). It examines the broader context to the management and control of children's homes. That context includes: the collapse in the number of residents during the last decade, an associated loss of purpose and direction, deficiencies in policy and management, a largely unqualified and inexperienced staff, and problems of control in homes.

2. A new Children Act comes into force on 14 October 1991. It is the most important piece of legislation affecting children* this century. Among other provisions, it both extends and clarifies the responsibility of the local authority for assisting children and families in need, and protecting and caring for children at risk.

3. The Act reflects a convergence of values about children as individuals in their own right, citizens enjoying legal protection, the parents of tomorrow's children and the future of our society.

4. It is essential that practice in relation to children in the public care reflects those values. Hitherto, in spite of best intentions, such children have often been disadvantaged and stigmatised. The duty of public care is to deal with those children as if they were our own.

CHILDREN IN CARE

5. 60,500 children were in the care of local authorities in England at 31 March 1990. This is a massive reduction on the figure of 95,300 recorded 10 years earlier. It reflects, in part, the success of preventive work by local authorities and others.

6. Children come into care in widely differing circumstances. A few have been abandoned as babies, some are in a crisis of adolescence, many have been neglected or offended against. What they have in common is a need for the care or control normally given by a parent, which cannot otherwise be provided.

7. Children in care are looked after in various ways. The greatest number (34,500) are in foster homes. Numbers in residential care declined by nearly two-thirds in the last decade to 13,200.

8. The halving of its market-share from approximately 40 per cent to 20 per cent arose in large part from considerations of philosophy and economy. Prevailing values in child care turned firmly in favour of placing children in families, and this was also usually perceived as much the cheaper course. The reduction also reflected changes in practice, such as the care order in criminal proceedings falling into disuse.

---

*I use the term "children" throughout to cover those aged 0-17 inclusive. I occasionally use the terms "young persons" and "juveniles" to denote older children within that age range.

RESIDENTIAL
CARE

ROLE AND PURPOSE

9. Is there any point in persevering with residential care? Can it be revived? My view is clear: residential care is, and under the Children Act will remain, an indispensable part of the range of provision for children in public care. Many adolescents make it plain that they prefer a residential home. The purpose of residential care should be to provide:

> a home for children who:

> ★   have decided that they do not wish to be fostered;

> ★   have had bad experiences of foster care;

> ★   have been so abused within the family that another family placement is inappropriate;

> ★   are from the same family and cannot otherwise be kept together;

> expert, multidisciplinary help with social and personal problems in a residential setting;

> containment and help in conditions of security.

Residential homes fulfil a specialist role as partners in a range of preventive and rehabilitative services designed to meet specific needs: observation and assessment, permanent family placement, juvenile justice projects, respite care for disabled children, and preparation for independent living.

10. It is plainly, however, in need of some sustained attention if it is to be equipped to play that role. Run down during the past decade, it is now overdue for re-investment in its management and practice.

THE INSTITUTIONS

11. Children in local authority care are accommodated in a bewildering variety of residential institutions. The great majority (80 per cent) are in community homes of various kinds, maintained or assisted by local authorities. The remainder are in voluntary homes or hostels, private homes, boarding schools (maintained or independent), NHS hospitals or units, mental nursing homes, and penal institutions.

12. The wide range of institutions used illustrates both a degree of differentiation in finding the most appropriate placement and an increasingly desperate search for a haven for troubled young people.

THE CHILDREN

13. Children in local authority care in residential establishments differ in some respects from the generality of children in care. They are older: 35 per cent over 16 and 70 per cent over 13. The proportion of children in residential homes who are over 16 is higher now than it was 10 years ago. Residential care is primarily a service for adolescents. That is the major factor in planning its future.

14. Children in residential homes have not been in care as long as the child care population overall: 40 per cent of them for less than a year. Turnover is unknown but is obviously substantial: more than 5,000 of the children who left care in 1988/9 left it from residential accommodation. The number experiencing residential care in the course of a year is obviously much higher than the resident population on any single day.

15.   The 1985 SSI Inspection of Community Homes identified many children who, in addition to family breakdown, had experienced sexual abuse, violence within the family, repeated rejection and numerous changes of carer before admission to local authority care. Failure to attend school was common and some committed delinquent acts; solvent misuse, misuse of drugs or alcohol, self-mutilation or suicidal episodes were noted.

16.   It is generally assumed that young people in residential care today present a greater concentration of difficulties than their predecessors. This may well be a consequence of the large reduction in the number of children in care overall. At the same time, however, the number of juveniles committed to care as the result of an offence has substantially diminished. The problems currently perceived probably arise from young people entering the system as a result of final breakdown in family relationships, or from adolescents already in care experiencing a crisis of disordered or challenging behaviour.

17.   Securing and co-ordinating the various services needed by these young people is extremely difficult. The Children Act and the Regulations and Guidance which flow from it provide a basis for improving services of various kinds to children in care. I have made recommendations elsewhere about planning and co-ordinating services.

WELFARE
OF CHILDREN

ADMISSIONS/ASSESSMENT

18.   Scrupulous assessment and review, requiring co-operation between a number of public agencies,is the basis of child care work. Children should not be placed in residential homes, even in emergencies or for assessment, without careful consideration of the alternatives and a positive decision that the residential placement is the best. Children should be asked to live in residential homes on the basis that this is a positive and jointly considered choice.

RIGHTS/COMPLAINTS

19.   Children's legislation makes certain rights explicit. Other rights are implied.

20.   Participation in decisions about the corporate life of a residential home may not be a right. To deny it, however, makes a powerfully negative statement about the valuation placed upon the residents by the controlling authority. Encouraging it offers them a status comparable to that of their contemporaries, and is itself positive preparation for that life after care in which these young adults make decisions for themselves.

21.   Children in homes should share in all the decision-making that goes on in families: about food, clothes, entertainment, holidays, privacy, furniture and decorations, pocket-money, control and discipline.

22.   The Children Act makes new, comprehensive provision for dealing with representations or complaints. But because young people may not be able to crystallise their feelings into an issue as clear-cut as a complaint, I conclude that the Department of Health might consider, in the light of the operation of the new complaints procedure, extending the scope of the new system of independent visitors (Schedule 2, paragraph 17) to all children in residential care.

23. The complaints procedure has been criticised as leaving the local authority ultimately to judge its own cause. I suggest that the Local Authority Associations consider offering an independent adjudication service where there is a continuing dispute between a child and his or her care authority.

CHILD PROTECTION

24. Children in residential care are vulnerable to exploitation by adults and to both physical and sexual abuse. Employers should offer protection in these areas by carefully scrutinising and, where necessary, investigating the credentials and antecedents of staff and of others, such as visitors and volunteers, who come into close contact with children in care. The local authority has substantial responsibilities in this respect.

25. The Children Act Guidance draws attention to the importance of consulting the lists kept by the Departments of Health and of Education and Science of people judged unsuitable for employment in this area.

26. Children may need protection from other children as well as from adults. Verbal or physical violence should always be treated seriously, and dealt with under the local child protection procedures.

EDUCATION

27. The educational difficulties that children often bring with them to care may be compounded by their experience of it, with crippling effects on their lives after leaving care.

28. Care authorities should act to remedy the educational disadvantage of children in their care, and do all that a good parent would do to ensure that children's educational needs are met.

29. Where Joint Sub-Committees are established between Education and Social Services Committees, they should include in their remit the task of devising and implementing strategies to meet the educational needs of children in care including those who have left school. The Department of Health should discuss with the Department of Education and Science the feasibility of issuing guidance to education authorities about the educational needs of children being looked after by local authorities.

LEISURE

30. Care authorities should ensure that constructive programmes, integrated with the local community, of leisure and artistic activities are available for all children in residential care. Full use should be made of all the facilities and opportunities offered by the Youth Service.

31. Attention should always be given to the cultural and spiritual needs and development of individual children.

HEALTH

32. The care authority is responsible, as a parent would be, for acting to ensure that the health needs, particularly in terms of monitoring and health education, of the individual child are met. It should also secure with the appropriate health authorities a local strategy for meeting the health needs of children being looked after. The Department of Health should require health authorities to co-operate with local authorities in producing plans for children's services.

33. I consider that social services departments and health authorities should reach local agreement on the provision of psychological and psychiatric support for children in care, which should be reflected in the community care plan. The Department of Health should consider whether a further review of those services is needed.

EMPLOYMENT AND AFTER CARE

34. Children in care, already disadvantaged educationally, may well have further problems in securing and keeping suitable jobs. Work is fundamental to a successful future for these young people. The care authority must address the employment needs of its young people individually and collectively, and use all means available to establish a secure base for their future working lives.

35. The deficiencies of after care have properly received much attention in the past decade. Too many children in public care have subsequently turned up in the population of penal institutions or on the streets. They should be enabled, not disabled, for adult life.

36. Plans for all children in care should be directed towards their self-sufficiency as adults. Preparation for independent living should be the focus of work with adolescents. Section 24 of the Act requires the local authority to provide after care up to the age of 21. Accommodation is central to a settled life: Section 27 requires assistance from housing as well as education and health authorities. Care authorities should seek to apply these sections fully.

37. Care authorities should include all the above elements (health, education, leisure, employment and after care) in care plans for individual children. They should invoke Section 27 of the Children Act 1989 in cases of difficulty in meeting the housing, educational or health needs of individual children. I support the relevant recommendation of the "Pindown Experience" Report (13.38) about the appointment of a named senior manager with specific responsibility for overseeing arrangements for the education, career development and working life of children in care, and recommend that it be applied generally.

ETHNIC MINORITIES

38. The needs of children from black and minority ethnic groups should be considered throughout every aspect of residential care: staff recruitment, training, placement decisions, monitoring, health and personal care, environmental and practical issues, preparation for independence, and after care.

CHILDREN WITH DISABILITIES

39. The Children Act will bring many children living away from home within new protective procedures. These children will include some with disabilities. I consider that, in the light of the operation of the new complaints procedure, the Department of Health should consider extending the scope of the independent visitor scheme to children with disabilities.

OFFENDERS

40. Only 2 per cent of the whole population of children in care are there on a care order made as the result of a criminal offence. Five per cent of the children in all residential homes are in that category. The proportion of children in Community Homes with Education subject to criminal care orders declined from 55 per cent in 1980 to 15 per cent in 1990.

41.   The criminal care order expires with the introduction of the Children Act, to be replaced by a residence requirement in a supervision order. Then, in due course, comes the diversion to the care system of young people previously remanded to prison.

42.   The position will soon be reached in which only the most serious or disturbed young offenders will remain in the care system, and in very small numbers. This poses problems of philosophy and management, particularly in relation to the needs of the large population of children in care whose offending records are similar to those of the average population. I conclude that, in developing their programmes on preventing crime, local authorities should consider the needs of children in residential care, and work with relevant community interests on preventive programmes.

43.   Some establishments must obviously specialise in working with offenders. I do not, however, advocate a policy of absolute segregation of offenders and non-offenders. Where they are to live in the same home, however, special attention should be given in assessment and review procedures to the needs of the non-offenders.

MANAGEMENT

LOCAL AUTHORITY POLICY/PLANNING

44.   Residential child care can be managed only as an integrated part of total child care provision. I am not satisfied that residential child care is at present an effectively managed resource.

45.   All social services authorities should have statements of policy for children's services, which provide the foundations for planning and managing those services, including residential care.

46.   I recommend that the Secretary of State should issue a direction requiring local authorities to produce and publish plans for children's services; and that the Department of Health should issue guidance on the content of these plans and monitor their implementation. I consider this to be necessary to secure effective planning and management of residential services. It will also assist implementation of the Children Act and provide a yardstick against which progress can be measured.

47.   Local authorities were, however, faced with a situation during the 1980s that was very difficult to manage. Residential care lost half its population in 5 years, and two-thirds in 10. It now cries out for a planned structure in which it can be seen as a positive resource within the range of children's services. Authorities should make full use of the residential services available, including those provided by voluntary organisations and other independent providers.

48.   Local authorities need to consider urgently whether they are still able to provide a full range of services to their young people, and how to form the necessary partnerships with other providers of all kinds if they are not. I consider that the planning process I have recommended will stimulate local authorities to deliver what is required.

LOCAL AUTHORITY MEMBERS

49.   The nature of the local authority's responsibilities as a parent makes it desirable that elected members retain personal oversight of the way in which they are discharged. Services for children - as for other vulnerable people - will have a keener personal edge and more adequately reflect the values of the community if they are led by elected members: without, of course, obscuring the accountability of senior managers, in particular of the Director of Social Services.

50. The way in which members exercise their oversight differs between authorities, and possibly among members. I doubt that a uniform pattern is necessary or desirable, but some authoritative advice would help members and, incidentally, their officers. I recommend that the Local Authority Associations commission or undertake such advice.

MANAGERS

51. The reduction in residential care during the 1980s, particularly rapid during the first half of the decade, precipitated frequent or regular reviews of children's services. 52. Residential care in any case presents difficulties of management and supervision. The physical isolation of an establishment from the management structure of its parent body may set it out of mind as well as out of sight. Maintaining occupancy at an optimum level, so that resources are fully deployed without being over-stretched, is a constant problem.

52. Residential care in any case presents difficulties of management and supervision. The physical isolation of an establishment from the management structure of its parent body may set it out of mind as well as out of sight. Maintaining occupancy at an optimum level, so that resources are fully deployed without being over-stretched, is a constant problem.

53. The effectiveness of the Children Act will depend in some -possibly large - part upon an effective residential sector as an essential ingredient of both preventive and remedial services. It is essential that the outstanding management issues concerning residential care are grasped by all managers with responsibilities towards it, from those managing groups of homes through to Directors of Social Services. Tightly drawn management structures, relying on carefully thought out information systems, are essential for effective monitoring. Roles need to be precisely defined and objectives set. The management line should include both professional experience of residential care and general managerial experience in the allocation and use of resources. I conclude that the management principles and techniques referred to in Chapter 4 of this Report should be extended to children's services generally; and that the Department of Health should issue guidance to local authorities to assist in this process.

54. Directors of Social Services should verify that their arrangements for managing residential child care within an overall strategy for children's services are effective.

MANAGEMENT/SUPERVISION IN THE HOME

55. The head of home is the biggest single influence upon it: in some cases, a determining influence upon its culture, ethos and practice. Heads of homes should be responsible for managing all the resources of the home, and should be equipped to do so by appropriate training, experience and supervision.

56. The functions of residential care require the head of home to be professionally qualified. This qualification will ordinarily be in social work, but there is scope in residential child care for people with qualifications in other disciplines to be appointed - with appropriate experience and training - as heads of homes. All heads of homes should be trained in management.

57. I commend the admirable Children Act Guidance on all aspects of staffing contained in Volume 4, Residential Care.

CONTROL IN THE HOME

58. A proper degree of stability or order in the life of the home is needed for its primary purposes to be performed. Achieving and maintaining stability and order is the outcome of numerous interactions: of policy, resources and management no less than of individuals and groups.

59. Formal processes of control may therefore have no more than a marginal effect overall, yet be critical at points when the presence or absence of skill and experience decides whether a combustible situation is ignited or dispelled.

60. The consent of residents to rules of group living and methods of formal control is important to their success. General guidance, however, is of limited use to staff confronted by challenging adolescent behaviour. They need to know what they can and should do, as well as what they are forbidden to attempt.

61. The subject of control in residential homes needs a new, positive approach. I recommend that the Department of Health, in consultation as necessary with other interested groups or individuals, notably the Central Council for Education and Training in Social Work, considers what further guidance and training on constructive measures of control in homes are needed.

SECURE ACCOMMODATION

62. I commend the Children Act Guidance on secure accommodation. But I note that at present there is no requirement for secure facilities other than in children's homes to be approved by the Secretary of State. This represents a gap in the legislation. I conclude therefore that all secure facilities should be subject to the approval of the Secretary of State.

63. The Home Office proposals for ending the remand of juveniles in penal establishments will, if implemented, make necessary an increase in the numbers of secure places available, which need to be evenly distributed across the country. I believe the Department of Health has action in hand to achieve these objectives.

OTHER PROVIDERS/INSTITUTIONS

64. Twenty per cent of children in residential care at 31 March 1990 were accommodated in institutions other than children's homes.

65. The use of a wide range of accommodation is to be welcomed where it is the result of careful evaluation of the individual child's needs and not faute de mieux.

66. Because responsibility for these homes is held by a number of different bodies I consider that the Government should now check that the regulatory procedures affecting children in residential placements other than in children's homes are suitable, and imply the same standards of protection where that would be justified.

SECRETARY OF STATE

67. The duty of protecting and looking after children is placed firmly by statute upon local authorities.

68. The Secretary of State's supervisory functions and responsibilities are brought up to date and extended by Part XI (Section 80-84) of the new Children Act. They include powers of inspection, inquiry, limited financial support, research, requiring returns from local authorities and acting if the local authority is in default; and a duty to review the adequacy of provision for child care training.

69. Section 7 of the Local Authority Social Services Act 1970 requires social services authorities to exercise their functions under the guidance of the Secretary of State, and Section 7A of that Act enables him to give them directions, individually or collectively.

70. The Secretary of State also has de facto responsibilities of answering to Parliament on child care matters, promoting national policies and representing the interests of the personal social services in the Public Expenditure Survey (a process described briefly in Appendix 5).

INSPECTION/REGISTRATION

71. Children's homes are the only residential service provided by local authorities not now subject to routine regulatory inspection. Regulation 22(4) of the Children's Homes Regulations 1991, which requires the local authority to cause each home to be visited monthly and reported on in writing, directs the authority towards fulfilling its management responsibilities. Inspection adopts a different perspective from management, is independent of management and applies its own particular methods.

72. Inspection is discussed at greater length in Part 2 of this report. I conclude that children's homes should be made subject to regulatory inspection by the local authorities' inspection units. This is contained in the Children Act Guidance. Nevertheless I recommend that the Secretary of State issue a direction to this effect.

73. It is important, however, that the particular needs of children and the parenting responsibilities of the local authority are fully acknowledged in the staffing and methodology of the inspection units. Staff with experience of children's services must obviously be deployed, and I recommend that membership of the Advisory Committees be extended and their independent element strengthened. The Department of Health should include guidance on these matters in its forthcoming guidance to inspection units on inspecting children's services.

74. The Social Services Inspectorate is already charged with monitoring the performance of inspection units, and this should apply also to their functions in relation to children's services. SSI should continue to inspect secure accommodation on behalf of the Secretary of State for the foreseeable future.

75. I can see no justification in these changed circumstances for voluntary homes continuing to be registered individually with the Secretary of State and inspected by SSI. I recommend that Section 60 of the Children Act be amended to cause voluntary homes to be placed on the same basis as children's homes for registration and inspection.

RESOURCES

STAFF

76. Staff are the principal resource of residential care and also account for 70 per cent of expenditure on it. The ratio of care staff to residents in community homes has improved dramatically: from 1:1.8 in 1979 to 1:1 in 1989.

77. The whole system of residential care depends upon the commitment and ability of its staff (the majority of them - historically - young women), many of whom are poorly prepared by training for the jobs they do. It is unquestionably wearing and responsible work. With residential care widely regarded as a placement of last resort, staff are said - not unreasonably - to be in a low state of morale. At the same time, every exploration of residential child care, every piece of research, every inspection continues to unearth examples of excellent practice. And young people themselves speak of the advantages and benefits of life in a residential home as compared with foster care.

78. I therefore very much welcome the inquiry the National Employers' Organisation for Local Authority Staff proposes to hold jointly with the Trades Unions into all the staffing issues surrounding residential care in local authorities. My report is, of course, restricted to residential child care, but I hope that my comments about the nature of the task, the qualifications needed to discharge it, and pay and conditions of service will both help the joint inquiry and stimulate further investigation.

PERSONNEL MANAGEMENT

79.   If the status and morale of residential care staff are to be restored to their previously high levels, a number of steps are required. Chief among them is the need for local authorities to establish forward-looking personnel management policies, designed to identify with precision the roles of different residential care staff and the relationships between them, in such a way that staff are clear about what is expected of them and the way in which they personally can develop. I recommend that managers set for unqualified staff clear objectives for personal development, for attainment within specific timetables. I conclude that the Local Authority Associations, or the Local Government Management Board on their behalf, should draw up guidance for social services departments within 6 months on staffing policy, personnel management and career development.

80.   One function of such personnel management policies should be a changed expectation of career progression. Residential care is used by some as a fast route into social work; others are content to stay put in their posts. Both situations have drawbacks. A point between the two needs to be reached. I conclude that the guidance referred to in the previous paragraph should cover this area too.

81.   The professional social work associations should demonstrate their leadership by devising policies for restoring the high status of residential care.

82.   The experience of this review reflects earlier findings that the nature of the task of residential child care establishes social work as its core discipline. This does not mean that every post should be occupied by a professionally qualified social worker, or that there is no place for other disciplines. All heads of homes, and ideally about one third of the staff, might need to be professionally qualified: the majority in social work, but with scope for the valuable contribution of professionals from other disciplines supported by appropriate experience and training. I conclude that local authorities should plan to secure within 3 years that all officers in charge of homes are qualified to DipSW.

83.   The remaining staff should be qualified at a level of the National Vocational Qualification appropriate to staff engaged in the complex task of caring for adolescents with difficulties. The work of care staff is no less important than that of those with a full professional qualification; staff management should set specific objectives for attainment within set timescales. The balance between the two groups of staff needs more discriminating assessment than I have been able to make, and is in any case a task more properly undertaken on behalf of the employing local authorities by the Joint Inquiry or by the Local Government Management Board.

PAY

84.   Basic salaries should be fixed according to qualification, with incremental progress for experience and satisfactory performance, and changes in salary levels should be linked with changes in these areas (or job content). The nature and responsibilities of residential work are such that there must also be a just level of remuneration for the unqualified staff on whom the service must depend for some time to come.

CONDITIONS OF SERVICE

85.   Both employers and staff have to recognise the reality of unsocial and inconvenient hours. Stereotyped systems of shift-working do not suit the task of providing care. The home secures increased continuity and clearer identity if a member of staff actually lives there. The Joint Inquiry might consider the basis on which a system of living-in that accords with contemporary values might be established.

LEADERSHIP

86. Pay and conditions of service are not the most serious matters affecting residential care; nor is training. The major problem is simply that the residential care of children is commonly regarded as an unimportant, residual activity. Thinking about it today is still dominated by historical attitudes towards looking after children: as women's work in which the skills are inherent or intuitive and the commitment of the workforce is exploitable.

87. The reality is very different. Residential workers are dealing with young people who may have been rejected by families, schools and employers; who are regarded as not needing or not being able to respond to health treatment; who have been grievously abused; who may be unloving as well as unloved, and behave badly. The skills and difficulties associated in this context with such concepts as care and control are exceptional.

88. The reality is also that advances brought about by improvements in pay, conditions of service and training will prove temporary unless they are co-ordinated within a strategy to improve the standing of residential child care as an occupation. Staff need to be assured that what they are doing is valued, important and will endure. That task is primarily for the employers and senior managers in the organisations that require and provide residential care. I trust that employers and the Joint Inquiry will address the issue.

TRAINING

89. The position set out by the survey of qualifications of care staff, reported in detail at Appendix 6, is not reassuring: 70 per cent of the staff currently employed lack a relevant qualification. It speaks eloquently of the low esteem accorded residential child care.

90. Comparisons with earlier years are difficult because relevant statistics are no longer collected. I fail to see how arrangements can be made for the planning and management of the social services workforce without the routine collection of relevant information on qualifications and training. I conclude that the Department of Health and Local Authority Associations should address the matter.

91. Such information as exists suggests that the proportion of staff in residential child care who possess a relevant qualification is no higher than it was ten years ago, which would mean, in fact, a net loss of trained staff from residential care.

92. Most of the causes of this are set out in the preceding section. In addition, residential work has always been seen as providing an apprenticeship for social work, and the majority of staff who have gained the Certificate of Qualification in Social Work have quickly used this as a passport to social work in the community.

93. This situation can be improved only within a strategy that makes residential child care an occupation of standing, that people want to join and stay in for a reasonable period in their careers. Training must be specifically addressed in the drawing up of the personnel management policies I advocate above. I recommend that residential child care be afforded priority in discharging the Secretary of State's duty under Section 83 of the Children Act to review the adequacy of child care training. I also recommend that the Department of Health, in consultation with the Central Council for Education and Training in Social Work and the Local Authority Associations, produce an action plan for securing within five years the number of qualified staff I suggest are needed: and establish an expert group to identify an appropriate content of residential child care within the Diploma for Social Work and the NVQ competences.

BUILDINGS

94. Physical aspects of the home are important to all who live in it. The strongest feature of residential child care, that it is primarily a service for adolescents, needs to be reflected in the buildings in which they live. A premium is placed on privacy, independence and choice, and this should extend as far as possible through all the physical aspects of the home.

95. A variable picture was presented of the state of maintenance, furnishing and decoration. Keeping these up to a good standard is obviously important. Badly maintained homes invite contempt of and by those who live in them. Allowing residents some choice on matters affecting them can only assist their development. Placing budgetary responsibility with the head of home is most likely to achieve the best use of resources.

MONEY

96. The provision of residential care services for children is expensive. Whether more cash is needed by these services rather than others, or by local authorities generally, are matters for the local authorities themselves and for central Government respectively.

97. Unit costs of residential child care have been rising in real terms throughout the past decade. I have identified factors which may account for this trend, and I do not consider that there is prima facie evidence of inefficiency in these areas.

98. The recommendations in this Report about qualifications and training will require additional resources. These, and any resource implications arising from further work and analysis, or future developments affecting the sector, will need to be addressed constructively by local and central Government through the normal processes.

THE FUTURE

CHILDREN ACT/DEPARTMENTAL PROGRAMME

99. One of the features of the Children Act and of the associated regulations and guidance is the extent to which they have utilised the product of the outstanding research into child care of recent years. Much of this is helpfully summarised for practitioners in two Departmental publications: Social Work Decisions in Child Care and Patterns and Outcomes in Child Placement. The changes brought about by the Children Act deserve careful evaluation. The Department of Health has planned its own programme, and I trust that other sponsors of research will ensure a suitable place for such evaluation in their own future work.

REGULATIONS AND GUIDANCE

100. I have carefully scrutinised the Children's Homes Regulations, and Volume 4 of the Children Act Guidance on Residential Care which was published in July 1991. I consider these to be excellent of their kind, promoting high standards of care in residential homes. I have commented in the text on the very few points at which they might be supplemented.

101. Their quality, however, does not itself guarantee that regulations will be observed and guidance followed. The Children Act will be launched after the most careful preparation; even so, it would be unrealistic to assume that the substantial weight of guidance accompanying it will be assimilated and implemented forthwith. The Guidance on Residential Care may be particularly vulnerable, given the sector's history of policy neglect and indifferent management, and the mobility and inexperience among its staff.

102. I therefore recommend, first, the Secretary of State should consider making periodic public reports of progress on implementation; and secondly that the Department of Health report to the Secretary of State in 18 months' time on the first year's operation of the Children's Homes Regulations and associated Guidance and institute such further arrangements for monitoring as then seem desirable. I have suggested elsewhere that the inspection units of local authorities might monitor at least part of the Regulations and Guidance.

THE WAY AHEAD

103. Residential child care should, within the framework set by the Children Act, provide, by the end of the century, for a largely adolescent population:

* ★ combinations of a home to live in, respite care and planned short-term accommodation;
* ★ in which personal and social development is encouraged and health, educational, leisure, employment, cultural and spiritual needs are provided for;
* ★ by staff who are appropriately trained and experienced for the task of preparing young people both for independent living and for re-integration into their families.

104. These are not unrealistic objectives. The new Act provides fresh opportunity for those with responsibilities for residential care to ensure that its value is proclaimed, that it is effectively resourced and that it is, above all, efficiently directed and managed.

MAIN
RECOMMENDATIONS

105. The report establishes that residential care is a necessary service for children - mainly adolescents - and sees its role and functions being enhanced by the effects of the Children Act 1989. The capacity of residential child care to discharge even its present responsibilities depends critically, however, upon improving its status as an occupation fulfilling an important purpose for important people - children in the public care.

106. Principal recommendations are given below: a chapter of conclusions and recommendations ends Part 2 of this report. The main recommendations are attributed to the bodies with, in my view, the principal responsibility for carrying them forward, but those concerning staff and training require the co-operation of a number of agencies.

107. LOCAL AUTHORITIES should:

107.1 address with urgency, individually and collectively through the Joint Inquiry or the Local Authority Associations (or Local Government Management Board):

★ establishing a system of career development and personnel management for residential child care staff;

★ increasing the numbers of appropriately qualified staff in residential child care;

107.2 ensure that residential care is planned and managed as an integrated part of children's services;

107.3 clarify, with the advice of the Local Authority Associations, the role and responsibilities of Members in relation to children in local authority care;

107.4 make sure that residential services are used at all times with the positive purpose of meeting the needs of children;

107.5 use the full scope of the Children Act, Regulations and Guidance to achieve the collaborative approach required to the health, education, leisure, employment and aftercare of children in care;

107.6 enable maximum participation by young people in care in all the matters affecting communal living.

108. THE JOINT INQUIRY should:

108.1 consider the balance required between residential child care staff holding the Diploma in Social Work and those holding the appropriate level of NVQ;

108.2 consider my comments about the special features of residential child care in reaching its conclusions about salaries and conditions of service.

109. THE DEPARTMENT OF HEALTH should:

109.1 secure, within the Government's overall strategy for social services training and in co-operation with the Central Council for Education and Training in Social Work and the Local Authority Associations, the improvements required in the training of staff for residential child care within 5 years; and establish an expert group to identify the appropriate content of training for residential child care within qualifying courses;

109.2 require local authorities to produce plans for their children's services and monitor their implementation;

109.3 complete the process of causing all children's homes to be routinely inspected by local authority inspection units by:

★ issuing the necessary direction and publishing the supplementary guidance envisaged, to include the functions and staffing of inspection units and membership of Advisory Committees; and

★ securing the appropriate amendment to the Children Act to transfer responsibility for registering voluntary homes to local authorities.

109.4 monitor the first year's implementation of the Children's Homes Regulations and associated Guidance and report to the Secretary of State;

109.5 review, with other interested groups, the legislation safeguarding the welfare of children across the full range of residential settings;

109.6 cause further guidance to be issued on the content of suitable training on constructive measures of control in homes.

CHILDREN
IN THE PUBLIC CARE

A REVIEW OF

RESIDENTIAL

CHILD CARE

PART 2

CHAPTER 1

INTRODUCTION

BACKGROUND

1.1   The "Pindown Experience" Report disclosed a disquieting situation about a large local authority's management of its community homes. Ministers took immediate action to ensure that the specific abuses identified in Staffordshire were not widespread. In addition this review was commissioned to examine, in the broader context, questions of control and management in individual homes or authorities.

1.2   There is continuing anxiety about residential child care on several counts:

★ the number of residents fell sharply during the 1980s, raising questions about its role and - more fundamentally - about whether it was needed;

★ there was an associated loss of a sense of direction, purpose and esteem;

★ there were gaps and deficiencies in local authority policies and management of residential child care;

★ the staffing was overweighted with unqualified and inexperienced people;

★ a concentration of adolescents among the residents posed problems of control which, if not handled appropriately, led to violence to staff and abuse of other residents.

1.3   I address these issues in this report. Resolving such well established problems is a matter of increasing urgency, and it has been one of the Government's main priorities in enacting the Children Act 1989 legislation and following it up with the regulations and guidance issued first in consultative form last year and in final and amended form last month as "The Children Act 1989: Guidance and Regulations: Volume 4 - Residential Care".

1.4   In my own review I have drawn on much valuable research done in the 1980s on children's residential care, and on Social Services Inspectorate (SSI) reports, which also influenced the 1989 Act and the subsequent regulations and guidance; but I have drawn, too, on valuable evidence given to me during my own review by those outside Government whom I saw, many of whom had already influenced the guidance when it was out for consultation.

1.5   My main conclusion is that the new legal framework, and the regulations and guidance which go with it, provide a radically new framework which, if fully used, should both oblige and help local authorities and others to address these problems effectively. My main anxieties focus on the imperative need for effective implementation within this new framework; and on issues of staffing, management and control which, as is usual in material directed to independent local authorities, the guidance does not address in great detail. And my main recommendations are designed to ensure that the implementation process is carefully monitored, with special regard to these key features. I attach as Appendix 1 a copy of the general approach in the regulations and guidance, as it is summarised in paragraphs 1.1 to 1.8 of the publication to which I have already referred. This shows the very high degree of congruence between my own analysis and the thrust of that guidance.

CHILDREN IN CARE

1.6 The responsibilities of Government towards children* rest on the ancient concept of the Sovereign as parent of the people, which is given effect in the statutory provision for promoting the welfare of children. Local Government has had a role in this since legislation of the Elizabethan era. Dr Barnardo and the other Christian charities invigorated the system with their programmes of child rescue in the late 19th century. The reforming Children Act of 1948 substantially increased the responsibilities of the State and established children's departments as free standing units within local authorities: to be reabsorbed when they became part of the new social services departments in 1971. The reorganisation of local government in 1974 left social services departments operating at the levels of county councils, metropolitan districts and London boroughs. These authorities continue to discharge the statutory duties of protecting and caring for children.

1.7 The number of children in local authority care continued to increase in the 1970s, but fell by nearly 40 per cent during the last ten years. At 31 March 1990 there were 60,500 children in the care of local authorities in England; ten years earlier there had been 95,300. The overall population of children declined during that period, but there was nevertheless a substantial decrease of 29 per cent in the number of children in care. Part of the reduction arose from changes in practice such as the virtual ending of care orders in criminal proceedings.

1.8 An important part of the reduction, however, is due to improved preventive work by social services departments. Local authorities succeeded, through providing appropriate services including social work, in maintaining many children in their own homes who might in earlier years have become separated from their families. There is now a higher threshold for admission to care, with the inevitable outcome that those who cross it are likely to have, on balance, a greater concentration of difficulties than their predecessors.

1.9 Various factors precipitate an episode in care (see figure 1). Very few children are abandoned these days; many more are neglected or abused. Delinquency is now rare as a reason for admission to care, being replaced by a constellation of issues surrounding breakdowns in relationship between adolescents and their families.

**CHILDREN IN CARE AT 31 MARCH
BY LEGAL STATUS, ENGLAND**

TOTAL NUMBER OF CHILDREN IN
CARE, 1980, 95,297

1980

TOTAL NUMBER OF CHILDREN IN
CARE, 1990, 60,469

1990

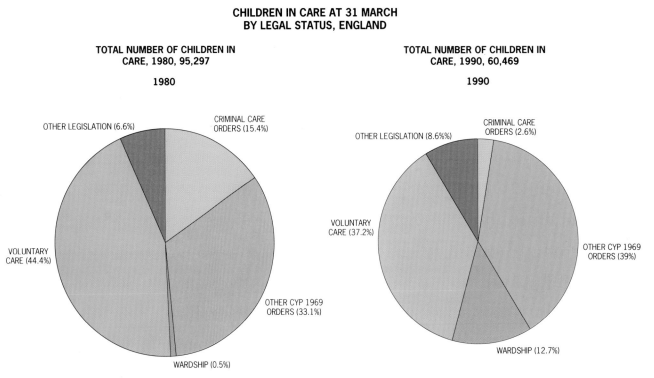

OTHER LEGISLATION (6.6%)

CRIMINAL CARE
ORDERS (15.4%)

VOLUNTARY
CARE (44.4%)

OTHER CYP 1969
ORDERS (33.1%)

WARDSHIP (0.5%)

OTHER LEGISLATION (8.6%%)

CRIMINAL CARE
ORDERS (2.6%)

VOLUNTARY
CARE (37.2%)

OTHER CYP 1969
ORDERS (39%)

WARDSHIP (12.7%)

CYP ACT INCLUDES CHILDREN REMANDED OR DETAINED IN CARE

figure 1 (paragraph 1.9)

*I use the term "children" throughout to cover those aged 0-17 inclusive. I occasionally use the terms "young persons" and "juveniles" to denote older children within that age range.

1.10 Some factors stubbornly endure, however: Bebbington and Miles (1),*
reporting on their study of 2,500 children admitted to care in 1987, found that
deprivation measured according to a range of indicators was strongly
associated with coming into care. The children admitted were often from
atypical families, in that only a quarter were living with both parents, almost
three-quarters of their families received income support, only one in five lived in
owner-occupied housing and over a half were living in "poor" neighbourhoods.
Bebbington and Miles compared the probability of admission to care of 2
children of similar age (5-9) but in very different social circumstances. By far the
more vulnerable had a one in ten chance of admission to care: arising from a
combination of a home with a single adult head receiving income support, the
family containing 4 or more children, the child being of mixed ethnic origin, all
living in a privately rented home with one or more persons per room.

THE CORPORATE PARENT

1.11 The Children Act 1989 (subsequently referred to as "the Act"), which
comes into force on 14 October this year, is the most comprehensive and far
reaching legislation about children and families yet enacted. Among other
things, it both extends and clarifies the duties of local authorities for protecting
children and promoting their welfare. It aims to provide:

★ help for children in need by supporting the family and working in
partnership with parents;

★ accommodation for children as part of a plan for their welfare;

★ the upbringing that a good parent would give to children committed to
the care of the local authority by the courts.

Throughout the legislation, the welfare of the child is the objective, and the local
authority must take into account the child's wishes in reaching decisions about
his or her future.

1.12   What constitutes a good parent, and whether a corporate body is
capable of acting as one, are fundamental and vexatious matters. The Act is
helpful on the first point by drawing together all the rights, powers, duties,
responsibilities and authority afforded to parents by the law into a new concept
of "parental responsibility". How this is exercised by natural parents is very
much for their discretion, subject to the minimum standards of care below
which criminal or civil action might follow, and the increasing capacity of the
child to make his or her own decisions.

1.13 The local authority acquires parental responsibility for children
committed to its care, and it has a duty under Section 22 of the Act to
safeguard and promote the welfare of any child it is looking after. This duty
must be exercised in consultation with the child and parents, and with
consideration of the child's religion, racial origin and cultural and linguistic
background. The manner in which the authority should discharge its parental
responsibility is further elaborated in The Children Act Guidance† to an extent
far greater than the parental responsibility of natural parents; reflecting the
need for a carefully structured approach when the care of a child depends upon
a corporate, public parent.

1.14 There are inevitable differences between natural parents and a public
body:

"The characteristics of parental love are that it is partisan, unconditional,
does not cease, does not have cut- off points, is long-suffering and does
not evaluate. The state cannot replicate this. Few parents are indifferent to
their children but the state, with its emphasis on fairness and equality,
cannot get too emotionally involved" (2).

*Academic references are listed numerically in Appendix 4 : Bibliography.

† I use this term to cover the various volumes of "The Children Act 1989: Regulations and
Guidance", published by the Department of Health.

1.15 The public parent is not necessarily a successful parent: In an inspection of community homes in 1985 by SSI, a study of cases revealed that each

"was rated on ten factors to give some indication of the local authorities' ability to act as a good parent, providing consistent and reliable parenting. In only 4 per cent of cases were there no elements of "failure" and in nearly 50 per cent of cases there were four failures or more" (3).

1.16 The Children Act Guidance, building on the Department of Health's earlier publication "Principles and Practice" (4), now sets out what is expected of state parenting. The obligations cover - of course - material well-being and provision for appropriate education and training, health care, employment, leisure and continuing interest and support after discharge from care. They also involve helping the child develop personal skills and preferences, a sense of personal identity and worth, a sense of security and an understanding of family life. This is not to replace or replicate the selfless character of parental love; but it does imply a warmth and personal concern which goes beyond the traditional expectations of institutions:

"Corporate parenting is not "good enough" on its own. Every child and young person needs at least one individual to whom s/he is "special", who retains responsibility over time, who is involved in plans and decisions and who has ambitions for the child's achievement and full development" (4).

1.17 Local authorities use a wide range of services for children in their care. They have looked traditionally to boarding out with foster parents and living in residential homes as the principal means of providing that "special" relationship for children in care. Cycles of fashion have led to alternating periods of dominance by foster care and residential home care. Both now operate in the context of values that place a premium upon keeping the natural family together and restoring it where possible if separation becomes necessary.

1.18 The current preference for fostering derives from:

★ a cluster of values about the family as the natural unit for bringing up children;

★ research evidence in the past of children remaining in residential homes who would have benefited from and needed family life;

★ the influence of reports by the Audit Inspectorate (5) and Audit Commission (6) which suggested that, if fostering was preferable for the child, it was also much less costly for the authority.

1.19 This preference has been expressed in such a way that the numbers of children boarded out have remained remarkably steady in the face of the large reduction in the overall number of children in care: 33,000 in 1978, reaching 37,000 in 1982, falling back to 34,500 in 1990. In the same period, the numbers in residential care have declined by 60 per cent (see figure 2).

CHILDREN IN CARE AT 31 MARCH 1980 TO 1990, ENGLAND

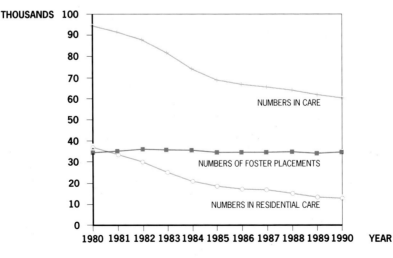

figure 2 (paragraph 1.19)

CHAPTER 2

RESIDENTIAL CHILD CARE

THE PROVIDERS

2.1   Residential care is difficult to define. For the purposes of this review I have taken it to mean continuous residence in permanently staffed accommodation for more than three children, which provides or enables access to the care and services normally available to children and such additional measures of care, control and treatment as resident children require. I have gone beyond this definition where I attempt to fulfil the wider remit of considering the position of children in care who are placed in institutions other than children's homes.

2.2   Children in care are currently placed in:

– Children's Homes - community homes provided by local authorities, some with observation and assessment, some with education on the premises; voluntary homes; private children's homes;

– Schools - maintained or independent boarding schools, often catering for special educational needs;

– Health Facilities - NHS hospitals or psychiatric units; mental nursing homes;

– Secure Institutions - youth treatment centres, penal institutions, or secure units in local authority community homes.

Information about the number of institutions accommodating children in care is poor, even for the children's homes. There are currently 81 voluntary homes registered with the Secretary of State; we estimate that local authorities in England provide approximately 1,000 community homes, and that there are around 100 private homes.

2.3   Department of Health statistics, compiled from returns made by local authorities, suggest that there were 13,199 children in care in these various settings on 31 March 1990 (the figure excludes children in private homes, for whom a separate return is not yet made). The great majority of these (10,490 or 80 per cent) were in local authority community homes. There were 1,188 children in care in special schools, 933 in voluntary homes, 204 in health establishments, 337 in prison department establishments and 47 in youth treatment centres (see figure 3).

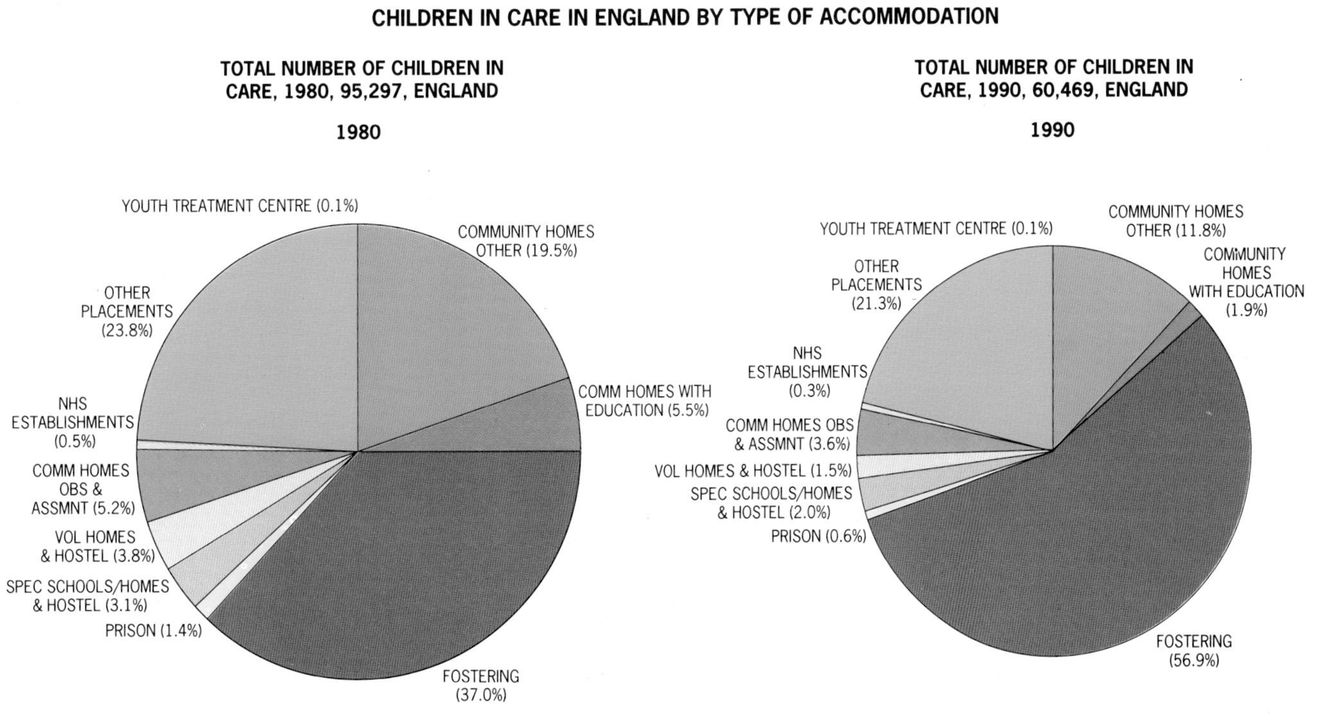

CHILDREN IN CARE IN ENGLAND BY TYPE OF ACCOMMODATION

TOTAL NUMBER OF CHILDREN IN CARE, 1980, 95,297, ENGLAND

1980

TOTAL NUMBER OF CHILDREN IN CARE, 1990, 60,469, ENGLAND

1990

figure 3 (paragraph 2.3)

2.4 As figure 3 shows, all these figures were lower than at the same point in 1985 and much lower than in 1980. They cannot reveal, however, the extent of use throughout the year. All the indications are that many more young people experience residential care during the course of a year than are in residence on any particular day.

2.5 Research by Rowe and others (7) on placement patterns in six local authorities established that residential care was still a significant part of the child care service. Placements were much higher than the "static picture provided by the annual returns" had suggested:

> "Residential establishments of one kind or another provided a third of all the placements made during the project and half of the placements of adolescents. Two out of five children and young people admitted to care during the project had their first placement in a residential establishment".

CHILDREN IN RESIDENTIAL CARE

2.6 The population of residential child care presents some interesting differences from the overall population of children in care in relation to such matters as gender balance (see figure 4), duration in care and factors precipitating entry into care. The principal difference, however, is one of age. Children in residential placements are generally much older than children in care as a whole (as figure 5 shows). The proportion of children over 16 in residential care has gone up from 22 per cent in 1980 to 35 per cent in 1990, compared with 24 per cent in the child care population. Seventy per cent of the children in residential care are over 13, compared with 42 per cent of all children in care. The older the child is on admission to care, the more likely it is that he or she will be placed residentially: 35 per cent at age 11, increasing to 50 per cent for those who begin care at 17. Berridge's study of children's homes in 1985 (8), along with the Rowe study, confirmed the statistical picture of a child population in residential care which was becoming increasingly older.

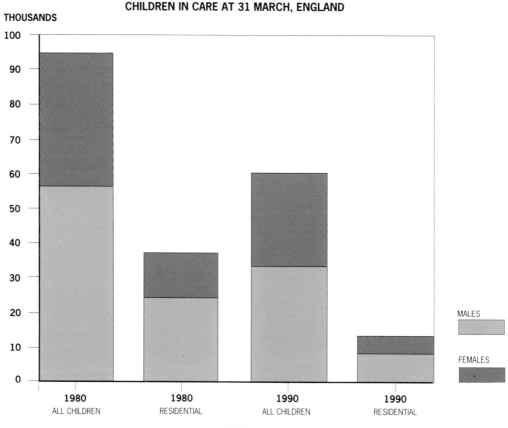

figure 4 (paragraph 2.6)

CHILDREN IN CARE AT 31 MARCH BY AGE

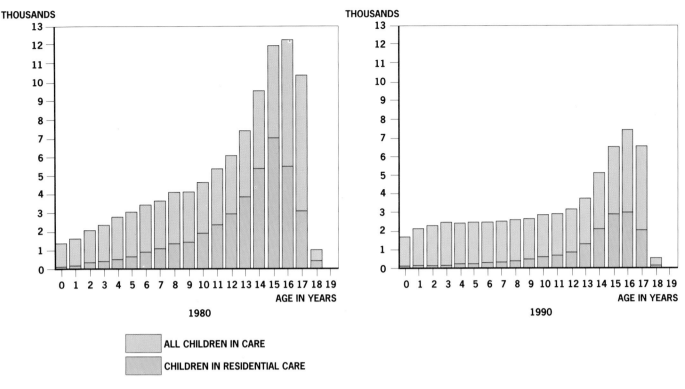

figure 5 (paragraph 2.6)

2.7 As numbers in residential care have declined, and authorities have increasingly emphasised placing as many children as possible in families, the impression has grown of homes becoming somehow residual, accommodating those children with behavioural or other characteristics which make them intrinsically hard to place. Rowe's study (7) reached the clear conclusion that:

> "residential establishments do indeed accept the more difficult youngsters .... We found that many problems were between 2 and 3 times more likely to be reported as "serious" for children and young people going into Children's Homes than into ordinary foster homes".

Berridge (8) found in some cases a long history of neglect or abuse and broken relationships.

2.8 Recent evidence collected from a sample of London authorities and voluntary organisations by the SSI suggests that, while some residents of children's homes do indeed present considerable difficulties in terms of behaviour and motivation, the extent of the problem can be overstated in relation to the general characteristics of the relevant age-group. At the same time research has shown that the residential care population is "a very diverse group in terms of age, gender, ethnicity and prior experiences" (9) although an experience of poverty is likely to be one thing the children have in common with each other and with the remainder of the care population. It appears nevertheless that children with long histories of disturbance or neglect, or with behavioural problems, are over-represented in homes.

2.9 Residential child care is now a service mainly for adolescents, and should be so organised, managed and provided. At the same time, there are important minority needs among its clientele. I deal elsewhere with the needs of children with disabilities and with young offenders. Considerations of race and culture run through all issues of child care in many urban authorities, and are therefore addressed here in general terms.

RACE AND RESIDENTIAL CARE

2.10 Concern has been expressed in the past about the possible over-representation of black children in care and of black adolescents in residential care in particular. The ethnic composition of the care population cannot be established with certainty in the absence of detailed monitoring.

2.11 Research evidence summarised in Patterns and Outcomes (10) suggested that younger African and Afro-Caribbean children were over-represented in admissions to care and Asian children were under-represented in all age groups. Among adolescents, only Afro-Caribbean young people entered care at a slightly higher rate than white contemporaries.

2.12 Black children were found by Barn (11) to be over-represented in care generally in her research into admissions in one London Borough in the late 1980s. Other research (1, 7) has not confirmed that children from particular ethnic groups are especially likely to be found in care, but has underlined concern about children of mixed parentage. Bebbington and Miles (1) found that:

> "Afro-Caribbean and African children are a little more likely to come into care than white children, but the differences are not statistically significant. On the other hand, a child of mixed race is two and a half times as likely to enter care as a white child, all else being equal."

2.13 The literature confirms that different needs of young people from minority ethnic backgrounds are not met by "cultural silence" (12) nor by the kind of white-centred social work practice described by Partridge (10). The recommended solutions are, in the main, well-known:

a.   recruitment of staff from minority ethnic backgrounds, and equal opportunities for training and promotion;

b.   training for all staff to cover, not just racial awareness, but practical techniques for meeting the different needs of young people from a range of backgrounds and cultures, and a range of experiences;

c.   placement decisions which reflect the need to promote identity and respect for black lifestyles, and combat isolation;

d.   preparation for independence and aftercare which is based on an understanding of the additional potential problems faced by young black people in a predominantly white society;

e.   monitoring, which will enable policies to be soundly based and effectively evaluated.

2.14 New evidence about the kinds of practice which work - for all children in residential care, not only black children - is expected to follow the Wagner Development Group's enquiry, which has commissioned from the Race Equality Unit of the National Institute for Social Work a study of the experience of black residential projects as a focus of good practice.

2.15 The new Department of Health statistical returns to be introduced with effect from 1 April 1992 will not include information on the ethnic background of children receiving services from local authorities. The Department is considering including such material in future returns. But whatever conclusions it reaches, I am convinced that it is essential for local authorities, as the service providers, to collect such data in order to inform both policy and operational decisions and to monitor their implementation. I have in mind particularly the take up of services, the ethnic composition of staff and the ability of service providers to accommodate the needs and wishes of minority users.

FUNCTIONS AND PURPOSE

2.16 The history of child care, emphasising the protection of children and the care of orphans, is inevitably reflected in the public image of the "children's home" - an image which has been slower to change than the needs of the children living there. The responsibilities of parents and of local authorities have now been clarified in the Children Act 1989. But the broader question remains:

how far can residential care supply what "home" does for children living with their natural parents? In 1985 Berridge (8), commenting on the family group home, said:

> " It has been criticized on a number of counts: it can never be 'a family'; that homes of this type cannot meet the needs of adolescents; and that it is not viable due to the size of the staffing group... It is important to emphasize that the term 'family group' now describes the staffing structure of these establishments, rather than perceptions of the children's residential experience."

2.17   Some authorities have attempted to clarify what they offer in the way of parenting to the children and young people who live in their homes. One authority, responding to the SSI survey of child care policy in 1987, included a statement about the nature of life in residential care in the policy document circulated to all staff:

> "There is a need to review the terms on which we offer care to children. Teenagers should not be deceived into believing that residential care is a substitute home with substitute relationships. What can be offered is security, shelter, consistency, concern, and preparation for adult life..." (20).

2.18   A similar range of factors was identified by Parker (13), from his review of literature for the Wagner Committee. Here he describes a framework for analysis of the parenting provided in residential child care, which had still to be elaborated by research:

> " He [Beedell 1970] goes on to suggest that parenting covers three main functions: holding (care, comfort and control); nurturing (the development of social, physical and intellectual skills); and the encouragement and maintenance of physical integrity (the whole person)."

2.19   But "parenting" is not a static or isolated concept. Well-documented changes in the family during the 1980s have implications for what society expects from the parental duties assumed by local authorities towards children and young people in their long-term care. The development of more flexible family forms may have encouraged the trend to regard a wide range of types of family placement as preferable to residential care. In future residential care should itself be seen as a flexible resource, providing privacy, a chance for recovery from stress, opportunities for retaining family links, and an initiation into independence.

2.20   What needs do homes in fact meet? Berridge (8) identified four main groups of residents in the homes he studied: emergency admissions; children waiting for new foster placements, or for whom foster placements had failed; adolescents with strong family ties; and the "long-term casualties" of the care system. He drew attention to the distress experienced by the younger children admitted in an emergency, or following placement breakdown. A number of studies have demonstrated the very significant impact of fostering breakdown on the need for residential care (see, for example, (14)).

2.21   The SSI inspection (3) of 149 "ordinary" community homes disclosed a variety of functions. Unsurprisingly, one in three described themselves as general purpose, catering for all ages and a wide range of need in the medium or long term. There were in addition 32 units for adolescents and 30 group homes, mainly long stay, for not more than 12 children. The remainder included homes containing more than one unit, each with a specialist task; homes specialising with particular difficulties, such as school refusal; homes providing short-term care; and pre-fostering units.

2.22   Homes were also developing outreach services or functions in which the home provided a base for other activities: day care for young children or holiday schemes, after care of former residents, work with groups in the community, respite care, intermediate treatment, and emergency services. A not unfamiliar picture emerged of vigorous evolution alongside depressed comments about homes becoming dumping-grounds.

2.23 The Wagner Committee (15) considered that residential care would continue to be needed for:

- ★ respite care, offering time-limited, planned relief to natural or foster families;
- ★ preparation for permanent placement, offering a planned, structured transition to new and lasting arrangements;
- ★ keeping families together, by accommodating siblings and preserving the links with the natural parents and other relatives;
- ★ care and control, in the small minority of situations where secure accommodation is the necessary option;
- ★ therapeutic provision, for socially and emotionally damaged children.

2.24 The most recent proposal about future functions comes from the London Boroughs Children's Regional Planning Committee (16). It identifies areas of care which residential units and related resources should provide, at least in part, as:

- ★ respite care for children with disabilities;
- ★ preparation for permanent family placement;
- ★ crisis intervention, assessment and care planning;
- ★ a home for adolescents for whom a family placement is inappropriate;
- ★ care and control (including secure accommodation) for young people with challenging or self-destructive behaviour;
- ★ supporting crime prevention strategies (for example, by bail support and remand);
- ★ family rehabilitation units, including mother and baby provision for very young women;
- ★ semi-independent accommodation preparing young people for leaving care;
- ★ housing with initial support for young people leaving care.

2.25 Parker (13) drew a distinction between the functions performed by residential establishments in relation to the wider welfare system and their primary aims in relation to the child. He showed how residential care performs the role of maintaining the system of foster care, by providing for transition, preparation and recovery; provides multiple functions in observation and assessment centres, including control and emergency care; and extended functions, by diversifying into day care activities:

"In an imperfect world, residential care often survives by virtue of these important wider functions rather than the course of its success in meeting the primary goals of individual children. Nevertheless, it should not be concluded that all wider functions are to be deplored, for in some instances these may enable another system, or part of a system, to operate in ways which encourage it to meet its primary goals more successfully in the interest of a child's well-being" (16).

Parker identifies primary goals as caring and rehabilitation; that is, returning to live with natural parents, preservation of family contacts, and education and preparation for independence.

2.26 More attention will be required in future to the expectations of the young people who live in residential homes. They have a right to a voice in decisions about them. Most adolescents, in or out of care, are likely to question or challenge situations they do not like or understand. As a last resort, young people in care may vote with their feet, run away, and take their chance on the streets.

2.27 The experience of this review suggests that young people expect a residential home to be above all homely, with all which that conveys about the physical circumstances of the home and the attitudes and outlook of the staff. They would like it to be small and the resident children a reasonably diverse group. It should provide opportunities for personal choice in decoration and furnishing, for privacy, and for private pursuits (including cultural) as well as group activities. It should be run in a way that promotes participation by young people in all the important decisions that affect the life of the group.

2.28 These expectations suggest a number of general principles, which are reflected explicitly in the Children Act Guidance:

★ the purpose of the establishment and the objectives for individual young people should be clear;

★ the home should provide an ambience in which residents feel valued, encouraged to want to stay and not to have to consider moving on too soon; and in which staff are willing and able to accept dependent relationships with children and young people;

★ the residents should have some influence over the regime; controls should be related to their needs as well as to the maintenance of the institution; trivial confrontation should be avoided;

★ the physical surroundings should be pleasant and comfortable and everyone should be interested in maintaining them in that condition.

CONCLUSIONS

2.29 The numbers of children in residential care fell dramatically within a sharp decline in the numbers of children in care overall. This has brought about a situation in which the continuing role and existence of residential child care is questioned.

2.30 Present reality appears to be that residential care is still extensively used, that occupancy on a particular day does not convey the extent of movement into and out of residential care, and that many - perhaps most - children in care have experienced residential placement at some time.

2.31 Building up a picture of what residential care should be used for starts with the needs of children and ends by balancing these against the availability of resources and the efficiency with which they are managed.

2.32 The characteristics of children in care suggest residential care as the preferred, best or only option in certain circumstances, where:

★ containment and treatment in secure accommodation is required for children who are a danger to themselves or others;

★ children have made considered decisions that they do not wish to be fostered;

★ children have had repeated bad experiences of foster care;

★ abuse has occurred within the natural family of such a kind that placement with another family is undesirable;

★ a complex of personal and social difficulties indicates a need for sophisticated and expert treatment in a residential setting;

★ children from the same family can be kept together.

I am pleased that the Children Act Guidance reflects these conclusions.

2.33 A service which meets such needs, and also fulfils the broader obligations of a local authority towards the children it is looking after, develops other positive purposes and functions: principally, as an important component of a range of services directed to specific goals, such as the expert observation and assessment of children, respite care for disabled children, juvenile justice projects, permanent family placement, and preparation for independent living. Associated with such purposes are some of the developments of family centres and outreach into the community.

2.34 The needs which residential care meets are characteristic needs of deprived and neglected children, and will continue. The Children Act offers new opportunities for preventive work in support of families. It also enhances the flexibility of residential care, by extending its boundaries with fostering on one side and with education on the other. It will, after 14 October, possess new shape, attributes and vigour. I should regard its future with confidence - provided the chronic problems concerning its status and staffing are at last resolved.

CHAPTER 3

WELFARE OF CHILDREN

3.1 This chapter concentrates on issues raised in the course of the review, and may not therefore cover all matters affecting the welfare of children in residential care.

ASSESSMENT AND DIFFERENTIATION OF PLACEMENT

3.2 Before a child is looked after by a local authority, an assessment must be undertaken to determine how his or her needs might best be met. The process of assessment, consisting of inquiry, consultation and evaluation, is best carried out where the child is living at the time. It should lead to a specific care plan, which should be kept under constant review through the period the child is being looked after. Good practice in planning and review is described fully in Chapters 2 and 3 of Volume 4 of the Children Act Guidance, and what follows is consistent with it.

3.3 Assessment and planning will first need to determine whether a child can remain in or be restored to his or her own family. If not, the choice lies between a substitute family or residential care. Consultation with the child is essential before a decision is made: many young people prefer residential care.

3.4 It is important that local authorities plan their residential care so that young people can be accommodated according to their different needs, taking account of their impact on other children. Some of the evidence put before me suggests that in some authorities residential child care provision has diminished to the point where placement options are so limited that children are placed wherever there is a vacancy. Such an approach prevents all but the crudest account to be taken of the impact of the placement decision on the young person concerned, or on the other children in the home.

3.5 On the other hand it is just as important to guard against too great an element of specialisation which could, through undue segregation, deprive children of the breadth of experience which would otherwise be available to them, and leave them vulnerable to stigmatisation as well as diminish their opportunities for maintaining family links.

3.6 It is difficult to find the right balance. I suggest certain principles which might be helpful:

    a.   the basic assumption should be that the least differentiation, the better. Children of different ages, needs and abilities can live together in care units offering good quality child care, appropriate to all children;

    b.   differentiation would be appropriate if a particular child requires specialised care which is available in only certain homes offering a regime of care, control and help to meet the child's assessed needs;

    c.   victims of abuse should be separated from children who are perpetrators of abuse;

    d.   children displaying persistent criminal behaviour should be kept apart from those who could be "detrimentally influenced" by them (but this does not imply strict segregation of offenders from non-offenders generally).

It should be for local authorities, in formulating their child care strategies, to determine the extent to which these principles can be applied, having regard to local factors.

3.7 Children needing to be looked after commonly display emotional distress and/or underdevelopment. It is then important for a psychiatrist or psychologist to participate in the assessment. This calls for close liaison between the appropriate health authority and the social services department.

3.8 The analysis of SSI reports suggests some social services departments have moved to manage admissions through the use of panels. Reports of their functions were generally favourable and planned admissions were possible. Otherwise admissions appeared to be controlled by the officers in charge, with or without specific criteria and the involvement of an external manager.

3.9 It is my view that rational placement decisions can be made only after assessment and through a panel or gatekeeping system which has an overview of resources available to the authority. The operation of this system would form part of the authorities strategic child care plan.

CHILD PROTECTION

General

3.10 Child abuse has become an increasingly common reason for a child being looked after by a local authority. A child who is a victim of abuse needs to be able to receive and accept care safely away from that abuse. A child abused by his or her family may not be able to accept that he or she can be protected by care in another substitute family. Residential care may be the best option for that child.

3.11 A child's need for protection may be covert. The need for care and control may be precipitated by a breakdown at home and at school which forces reception or committal to care. After placement, when the child feels sufficiently safe with care staff, he or she may disclose information about abuse within the family. Whatever the formal reason for care the child should then become the focus of the processes of child protection.

3.12 Some children or young people who have been abused or disclose abuse may wish simply to be well cared for by staff who are aware of this background. Others will be affected by the abuse in such a way that their behaviour becomes challenging. Dealing with this is specialised work and should be carried out only in those homes which are adequately staffed with qualified, experienced and skilled personnel supported by reputable external professional consultants.

3.13 An analysis of SSI reports undertaken for this review draws attention to the gap between the therapeutic aspirations of homes in this respect and the lack of adequate competence and skills on the part of the staff of the home. The term "counselling" was frequently used by staff to describe talking and listening to children privately. This activity is an essential part of looking after any child and to invest it with therapeutic significance is to isolate it from the basic craft of child care.

Detection of abuse

3.14 The child protection requirements on staff in children's homes and independent schools are set out in the Children Act Guidance. The specific guidance on child protection contained in "Working Together" (17), which covers both the maintained and the independent sectors, is currently being revised and will include a chapter dealing with residential care. These sources of guidance serve to integrate residential child care into the network of agencies coordinated by area child protection committees.

Abuse by residents

3.15 Children in residential care are sometimes abused by other children in the same home. Abuse of this sort should be dealt with under the local child protection procedures. This is an important safeguard for vulnerable children in residential care which opens the processes of the home to proper scrutiny and review. Inappropriate tolerance of a sub-culture of violence or of sexual behaviour demonstrates a fundamental lack of respect for the children concerned.

3.16 The potential for abuse of one child by another is an important consideration. It is clearly undesirable for victims of abuse to be placed with young people who have abused others.

This has implications for placement decisions and requires authorities to make available an adequate range of facilities.

Abuse by staff

3.17   Abuse by staff is covered in the Children Act Guidance. It is in the interests of the establishment to be seen to be open and co-operative with the police and social services. However good the checks employed in the selection of staff there can be no guarantee that staff will not abuse children placed in their care. Consequently there must be management machinery in place which can detect abuse and be alert to the potential for abuse: for example, no child should be allowed to have an exclusive relationship with one member of staff. A climate needs to be created in which the possibility of abuse by staff is realistically acknowledged by children, staff, management and indeed the general public. Children must feel able to confide in trusted members of staff. Junior staff must feel able to report evidence which may implicate more senior staff. At the same time staff feel vulnerable, in a context of heightened awareness of abuse, to accusations of misbehaviour. Employers should make clear that appropriate physical contact with children in care continues to be desirable.

3.18 I welcome the Children Act Guidance which recognises that all children in all types of residential child care establishment must have access to a telephone which they can use in private and which has prominently displayed the telephone numbers of child care helplines, independent visitors, the social services department, the police etc. Complaints procedures (see paragraphs 3.47 ff) are necessary but, for a child in residential care, they are not sufficient. The child will know only that he or she has a very serious problem which he or she needs to talk to somebody about, however difficult that may be.

3.19   The development of institutionalised practices may lead to staff losing awareness that what they are doing constitutes a form of abuse. This may well be the case where the practice arises from a new 'philosophy' or method of care which has not been exposed to external scrutiny. Ingrained cultural attitudes may predispose some male staff to adopt attitudes towards young women which may be highly discriminatory and demeaning and lead on to child abuse. Management must be aware of gender issues, deploy male and female staff carefully and ensure that methods of care and control are appropriate.

Checks on people having access to children

3.20   The "Pindown Experience" Report described how men who had convictions (including sexual offences) had visited young people in children's homes. Although the report found no evidence that the men had abused or attempted to abuse any children, they were clearly undesirable associates for the children. We know, from other cases, that paedophiles behave in a predatory manner towards vulnerable children in residential care.

3.21   The potential for abuse by staff and visitors raises the question of police checks. Access by care agencies to police information on criminal convictions is a difficult matter which raises issues of cost, organisation and priorities as well as civil rights. Volume 4 of the Children Act Guidance already draws attention to the importance of consulting the lists kept by the Department of Health (for social services) and the Department of Education (for schools) of people judged unsuitable for employment in these fields; and emphasises the responsibility on authorities and others running children's services to check the suitability of those employed in them or otherwise in contact with the children. The "Pindown Experience" Report made a number of recommendations in this area which are being pursued actively by the Government Departments concerned.

HEALTH AND EDUCATION

3.22   At the point at which children are looked after by a local authority, their health may already be a cause of anxiety. The 1985 SSI (3) report made seventeen recommendations about the health care of children. In the survey of SSI reports conducted for this review, though there were instances where the provision of health care was considered adequate, there was evidence that the process of health assessment generally was haphazard and the use of medical services was largely in response to illness. Despite routine medical examinations there was little concern with prevention and health education. This seems to me to be unsatisfactory. Volume 4 of the Children Act Guidance makes clear that programmes of health education and health care should be set up as an important part of the care package offered to children in homes, and reflected in the statements about the homes which will be produced under the Act, and I endorse this approach. In particular, in the light of recent concern about a private nursing home, I call attention to paragraphs 2.30 - 2.32 of that Volume, which deal with the important issue of consent to the medical examination and treatment of a child.

3.23 That children in care underperform educationally has been established most recently in the work of Sonia Jackson (18). This conclusion remains valid in spite of the efforts, noted in SSI reports, that residential care staff make to create close links with schools. Children who have experienced disturbance and disruption in their early lives are likely to come into care already educationally disadvantaged. It is even more important, therefore, that educational deficits are identified and made the special focus of attention by care staff. Educational attainment is one means by which children will be strengthened to cope with independence.

3.24 Care authorities should act to remedy the educational and health disadvantage of children in their care, and do all that a good parent would do to ensure that children's educational and health needs are met. Securing effective health and education services for children being looked after requires not only much effort by residential care staff but also a commitment to the needs of residents by the education and health authorities. That commitment starts during the assessment process, when psychological and/or psychiatric input may be required. Following placement, there needs to be agreement between those providing the home and the appropriate health (both District Health and Family Health Service Authorities) and education authorities about the level and quality of support in these areas which is offered to the home's residents. This support should be carefully planned and recorded in each home's statement of objectives, as the Children Act Guidance states.

3.25 Strong representations were made to me about the difficulty of securing psychological and psychiatric support in dealing with some extremely troubled young people. I have not been able to evaluate the cause for concern, but it would be appropriate for local agreements to be reached by social services departments and health authorities in their community care plans about the need for and provision of such support for children being looked after. I conclude that the Department of Health should consider whether a further review of those services is needed.

3.26 Section 27 of the Act requires local education, health and housing authorities to help local authorities discharge their responsibilities towards children "by taking any specified action". That and the following section impose reciprocal obligations on education and social services authorities to co-operate. Where necessary this requirement should be invoked.

3.27 Where Joint Sub-Committees are established between Education and Social Services Committees they should include in their remit the task of devising and implementing strategies to meet the educational needs of children in care including those who have left school. The Department of Health should require health authorities to co-operate with local authorities in producing plans for children's services; and should discuss with the Department of Education and Science the feasibility of guidance to education authorities about the educational needs of children being looked after.

LEISURE

3.28 Leisure should be creative and happy for young people. Where leisure and artistic activities are organised on a collective basis, great care should be taken to avoid institutionalisation. Individual attention is needed to a child's leisure, as to other activities, and opportunities for private pursuits should also be encouraged; children's homes have been criticised for limiting children's horizons by not providing a sufficiently stimulating environment intellectually, aesthetically or spiritually. Youth and education services may have a particular contribution to make, and authorities should where possible refer to them in their plans for children's services.

EMPLOYMENT AND AFTER CARE

3.29 Employment can be a problem for children entering care in adolescence and for those reaching adolescence in care. Fewer than 30 per cent of the 368 children over school-leaving age encountered in the 1985 SSI Inspection were in further education or employment. Parker (13) endorses this very bleak picture. But unemployment is not inevitable: there is also evidence that some homes can achieve better employment prospects than others. Being without work produces additional problems while in care and becomes acutely disabling at the point at which a young person should be becoming self-sufficient. Continuous and determined efforts are required by the authority to assist its young people to find and retain appropriate employment. Section 24 of the Act will require the local authority to provide after care to any child ceasing to be looked after by them, up to the age of 21, and section 27 requires assistance from housing as well as education and health authorities. Good parents do not sever all connection with their children on their 18th birthdays.

3.30 The qualitative study of young people leaving care by Stein and Carey (19) provided one of the first systematic accounts of the situation facing a representative group of 45 care-leavers. The study showed the limited amount of preparation and support available to the young people as they embarked on independent life, which compounded rather than compensated for the disadvantages they had experienced in childhood:

" In comparison with young people who had not been in care, our young people were more likely to be unemployed, to lack educational qualifications, to be living in poverty, to change accommodation frequently and to be confused about their pasts and unsettled in their present relationships. At its worst, the state had become an added burden rather than a supportive parent."

3.31 There is some evidence that this and other research had an impact, at least on the policy-making levels of social services departments. The SSI study of policy statements, collected from English local authorities in 1987/88, records that in

"42 documents - that is, in documents from about two-thirds of the authorities which sent in any - there is specific reference to the need for policies which aim to prepare young people for independence...several set the discussion in the context of recent research findings.."(20).

The documents concentrated on three broad areas of preparation: at the 14+ stage, in the period immediately surrounding the date of leaving care, and continuing support in the background in the months that follow.

3.32 Despite the evidence from these documents that the problems of leaving care have been widely identified, subsequent research has continued to emphasize the lack of effectively implemented solutions. Both Garnett and Bonnerjea (reviewed in (10)) draw attention to "the gulf between the current position and what is really required.." It is this gulf which the provision of the Children Act is designed to fill. Evaluations of leaving care schemes (see, for example, (21)) have also provided practical recommendations for social work managers. Two factors stand out as central to success in preparing young people: first, the need to build preparation into planning throughout the teenage years; secondly, the need to establish genuine co-operation between departments, so that housing, education, training and income support can all be tackled in a co-ordinated way. All of this implies the need for policy co-ordination between Departments and new demands on social work time and expertise.

3.33 The Children Act Guidance makes clear that local authorities should of course take account of all these factors in their care plans for individual children, and that residential homes should establish and keep links with health, education, leisure and employment services. I endorse this. These matters are of such intrinsic importance, however, that arrangements for them should receive additional oversight at senior management levels and be reported regularly to the Social Services Committee. The "Pindown Experience" Report recommended (13.38) that:

"there should be a named person at senior management level with responsibility (a) for ensuring that care and attention is given to the education, career development and working life of children in care, and (b) for the consideration of any policy or practice issues".

That proposal seems to me to have general application: local authorities should place the responsibility for reviewing the subjects specified by the "Pindown Experience" Report and by this section of my report on a named senior manager, and require regular reports on the operation of the arrangements involved.

CHILDREN WITH DISABILITIES

3.34   A number of categories of children are not identified specifically in this report. My conclusions are intended to apply to all children, but a few words might usefully be said about children with disabilities.

3.35   Government policy since 1981 has been that no child should grow up in a large mental handicap hospital. I note the success of this policy. Numbers of children in such hospitals have fallen consistently and in 1989 11 of the 14 regions had no children in large mental handicap hospitals.

3.36   Those children with disabilities for whom accommodation has been arranged and paid for by social services departments will, on 14 October 1991, become children looked after by the local authority. The number of children who will be affected by this legal transition is unknown because there have been no statistical returns which identify child residents other than those in care. However when the new Act comes into force new methods of statistical returns will operate which will include these children. In addition individual authorities will be required to keep a register of children with disabilities (Schedule 2(2)). These measures will mean that children with disabilities living in residential care will become much more visible as a group with special needs.

3.37   The particular vulnerability of children living in residential care is discussed elsewhere in relation to child protection and complaints procedures. This vulnerability is compounded in the case of children with disabilities. A child lacking mobility may be totally dependent upon those providing physical care and may be unable to ward off physical or sexual abuse. Such a child may not be able to communicate except through a trusted and skilled intermediary. A child with a learning disability may have no understanding of the significance of being abused save the personal distress experienced. Because children with a disability may be prone to injury or have an atypical developmental pattern, the detection of abuse becomes much more difficult. Furthermore, physical signs which could appear to be signs of abuse may have a benign explanation.

3.38   These special vulnerabilities, and the necessarily intimate relationship between the child with disabilities and the staff in these homes, imply an extra burden of responsibility and place on staff an extra vulnerability to accusations of abuse. Any safeguards that can be built in to ensure better protection of children with disabilities should be welcomed by the staff as well as the children and their families.

3.39   It may be hard for a child with disabilities to obtain effective access to a complaints procedure. Using telephone helplines may be difficult because of problems with oral communication and the limitations on privacy imposed by severe immobility. I consider therefore that consideration should be given, in the light of the operation of the new complaints procedure, to extending the appointment of independent visitors to children with disabilities. Such visitors, who would need appropriate communication skills, would play a particular role in relation to protection from abuse and access to representation and complaints procedures.

YOUNG OFFENDERS

3.40   A phenomenon of the 1980s was the great reduction in the former approved school population within residential child care. This reduction, which itself led to a decreased demand for residential care, arose from reaction against the philosophical approach embodied in the Children and Young Persons Act 1969. That Act (although unimplemented in some major respects) sought to establish local authority care as a major means of dealing with juvenile offenders on the basis that the same roots produced both delinquency and social deprivation. The reaction against it took two forms: scepticism about the effectiveness of care in changing delinquent behaviour, and representations on the basis of justice (or equity) that a "sentence" of care could be wholly disproportionate to the offence and more punitive in its effects than a straightforward sentence.

3.41   When the Children Act is brought into force, it will no longer be possible to make a care order on the grounds of a criminal offence. It is important to register this change forcibly, since a principal stigma borne by children in the public care is caused by the misapprehension that their status arises from criminal behaviour on their part. What remains is a tiny minority of very serious offenders detained under Section 53 of the Children and Young Persons Act 1933. They will be added to by a new provision of the Children Act, which will enable courts to include a residence requirement of up to six months into a supervision order made in criminal proceedings. The ending of remands of young people to prison means that a population hitherto deemed too unruly for local authority care will also be directed to it.

3.42   These changes have the paradoxical effect of requiring the same care system to look after small but significant numbers of seriously criminal adolescents by the side of a much larger population whose social and personal difficulties, while extreme in some cases, have not led to convictions for such serious offences. This larger population is by no means wholly non-delinquent, and the behaviour of some of its members may create even more anxiety than that of young people who have been convicted. But the administrative and judicial distinctions between offenders and non-offenders have in recent years heavily emphasised justice and punishment for the former and welfare and care for the latter, to the point at which arguments might reasonably be advanced for separating remanded and convicted young people from others in residential care.

3.43   I conclude that any such general requirement would be unnecessarily onerous upon the whole population of remanded and convicted children, further fettering the judgement of the responsible authority and obstructing desirable transfers from closely controlled to more open environments. Careful assessment of individual need in relation to all the options available is required in such circumstances, and the responsible authority should give particular weight to the interests of any non-delinquent children involved (some principles have been suggested in paragraph 3.6 above). The developments envisaged in relation to offenders and young people on remand will require additional residential provision of a specialist nature: providing secure accommodation or other residential facilities with programmes that concentrate on changing patterns of delinquent behaviour.

3.44   The prison statistics for England and Wales show that the number of juveniles in prison establishments has fallen significantly since 1985, from 1,196 to 572. However, it is also known that a significant proportion of young adults in prison have previously been in care. Children in care may be at risk of becoming delinquent because of a variety of factors; children in residential care are in any case in the age group in which most delinquent behaviour occurs. I conclude therefore that, in developing their programmes on preventing crime, local authorities should consider the needs of children in residential care along with other children in their area, and work with relevant community interests - including voluntary organisations - on preventive programmes of education, leisure and employment.

3.45   This overall reduction of offenders in the care and penal systems is one of the success stories of the last decade, owing much to the work of local authorities and voluntary organisations as well as to the extension of police cautioning and diversion from the penal system. The steps outlined in the previous paragraph are needed to arrest the progress of some young people from residential care into the penal system.

THE RIGHTS OF CHILDREN

3.46 The Children Act 1989 embodies a new framework of children's rights, which inform the various volumes of Children Act Guidance. This is a major and welcome development, and one which provides the foundation for the approach taken in this report. Some of the rights are expressed positively, for example the right of the child to express his or her opinion freely and to have that opinion taken into account; others are expressed as protections, for example against abuse. The next section deals with the general protection afforded by complaints procedures.

COMPLAINTS

3.47 The Children Act makes new, comprehensive provision for dealing with representations or complaints. I welcome the Children Act Guidance in this area, in particular the requirement for involving an "independent person" at every stage.

3.48 In every residential home there should be a culture which encourages and supports staff in listening to children, taking on their distress and acting to resolve it. I am concerned that under the formal procedure in the Act a child needs to formulate what has happened as a complaint and to know of the existence of a complaints procedure as well as how to activate it. I have received evidence, which I have found persuasive, that a child needs someone with whom he or she can talk through the problem before a decision is made on how best it might be handled. I conclude that the Department of Health should, once the operation of the new complaints procedures under the Act has been evaluated, consider how best to meet this point. In doing so the Department might consider whether there is scope for developing the role of the independent visitor in relation to children in residential care, and in particular to children with disabilities (see paragraph 3.39).

3.49 Even when a complaint is upheld, the local authority is not bound by the outcome. Complaints procedures cannot be a complete answer when the authority, in response to a complaint, still falls short of discharging its parental responsibility towards a child. The role of the independent person within the complaints procedure is limited to the influence which that person can bring to bear upon an authority.

3.50 The Commissioner for Local Administration will be able to examine allegations of maladministration in relation to the handling of complaints, but the substance of the complaint may not be accessible. I suggest that the Local Authority Associations consider offering a service of independent adjudication in cases of intractable dispute between a child and his or her care authority.

CONTROL

3.51 One feature of residential child care has changed little in the past decade: the obsession with maintaining control within the establishment. A DHSS Working Party on Control and Discipline in Community Homes (22) reported in January 1981 in terms which still ring true:

> "Problems of control and discipline arise from deficiencies in the child care "system" and those who work in it as well as from the behaviour of individual children. Improving policies, objectives, resources, professional practice, management and supervision will substantially reduce the difficulties encountered. Anxiety about control and discipline is at its lowest where the primary purpose of the home is to assist in solving the personal and social problems of the residents, and where the collective efforts of all involved directly serve this purpose. The unavoidable difficulties which arise will be best dealt with by staff exercising their own judgement within a framework of clear policies and planned procedures".

3.52 Two aspects of control in particular continued to cause anxiety throughout the decade. An increase in reports of violence against staff in a range of helping occupations was reflected in social work in both residential and community settings. A DHSS Advisory Committee under the chairmanship of Lord Skelmersdale published *Violence to Staff* (23) in 1988; the factors associated with violence against social services staff received further attention from employers, professional associations and unions.

3.53 Residential care staff need to acquire the confidence to be able to handle situations of potential violence. Part of this is the assurance that other staff are on hand. Part of it must also be a knowledge of how to respond. Training in conflict avoidance and the management of aggression is important. Some children in certain defined circumstances will need to be physically restrained and staff should be trained to do this in a way appropriate to child care. But even more important is training in approaches which reduce the incidence of violent behaviour.

3.54 The second disturbing feature concerned running away and other forms of unauthorised absence. These were a focus of concern in both the 1981 Report on Control and Discipline (22) and the 1985 Report by SSI on Community Homes (3). Running away should always be treated seriously but the response to the individual should be carefully managed to avoid the child feeling like a fugitive. Children come into residential homes so that they can be cared for and protected. By running away children explicitly reject that system. Widespread or frequent running away requires investigation by the authority.

3.55 Millham and colleagues at the Dartington Social Research Unit undertook a major study of boys in approved schools in the 1970s (13) and found that the *level* of control, rather than its style, was a key variable associated with absconding. De'Ath (24) has pointed out that running away from homes of all kinds is by no means a new phenomenon: it was estimated in the mid-1980s that approximately 80,000 young people went missing in Great Britain each year.

3.56 One important finding from the Central London Teenage Project - a "safe house" for young runaways - is the high proportion of children formerly looked after by local authorities who have appeared among the people seen by the project (one third of the total in the first two years of operation). One quarter of those admitted to CLTP had run away from care (25): - "over half...were persistent absconders and had already run away at least five times before going to the safe house". The reasons they gave for running away included: the fact that their placement had been too far from home; they had been in a temporary placement for assessment too long; no one had taken an interest in them; they disliked all the rules and regulations, and they felt stigmatized by "being in a Home". A further reason given by two young people was that they were alarmed at the prospect of imminent "independence" (25). Similar reasons have been reported by the Children's Society from the experiences of their 'refuges'.

3.57 Guidance and regulations, professional advice and research all counsel against creating the situations which these young people cited as intolerable. Yet this does not, of course, explain why some people run away from these situations and others do not. Apart from individual characters and personal histories, part of the explanation may lie in the control regimes operated by homes, as the Dartington study suggested. Berry's work on residential care for children in the 1970s explored the methods of discipline used in between forty and fifty establishments (26). She comments that, although the

> " - method of welcoming back absconders, with runaways knowing that whenever they returned they would find food awaiting them and a warm bed, is not only expedient in the short run but a far more effective way of handling actual and potential absconders - "

logic often has very little to do with it (27). Staff in homes, like everyone else, can act irrationally and angrily in stressful situations. This in turn argues strongly for the need for staff support and supervision, if the home's policy on control is to be followed through in practice.

3.58 Residential staff undoubtedly feel under considerable pressure on at least two counts in addition to their understandable anxiety about personal safety. In the first place, the consequences of any loss of control may impinge upon the neighbourhood, and are likely to become the focus of controversy as the "failings" of a publicly-provided and politically-controlled service. Secondly, there is an understandable feeling that, while antiquated and inappropriate methods of physical control have quite properly been forbidden, staff have had very little help, advice or training in better methods to replace them. Section 8(2) of the Children's Homes Regulations 1991 lists prohibited measures of control, and sections 1.82-1.92 of the Children Act Guidance elaborate on these and offer constructive guidance of a general nature.

3.59   I conclude nevertheless that residential staff as yet receive insufficient preparation and training for those aspects of their task that relate to the maintenance of a controlled environment. More work is needed: for example, on the use of authority in professional relationships, the participation of residents in formulating and reviewing the code of conduct for the home, and - where necessary - the use of methods of physical restraint. Further work should be initiated by the Department of Health as a result of the new Regulations; and should concentrate, in consultation with other interested groups or individuals, notably CCETSW, on what further guidance is needed on the content of training in constructive measures of control.

CHAPTER 4

MANAGEMENT

INTRODUCTION

4.1 Every service needs to be delivered within a well-planned and well-managed structure if its objectives are to be achieved economically, efficiently and effectively.

4.2 From the "Pindown Experience" Report comes a picture which reveals, in Staffordshire, the absence of both planning and management. The delivery of residential services to children was "related more to crises than careful and well-informed planning" with "little sense of direction" (para 17.21). Criticisms were directed at the performance of managers at different levels within the social services departments: "... senior management was perceived as making decisions in isolation, without adequate consultation or information gathering ..." (para 17.8). Moreover, "... it was almost impossible to get through the layer of middle management to communicate with top management" (para 17.14). The Report concluded (para 17.34) that: "the management of Staffordshire social services department contained numerous negative elements. Radical change is needed ... if the department is to be more effectively managed in the future".

4.3 Thankfully SSI reports show that the Staffordshire picture is an extreme one, with many social services departments managing child care policies in a satisfactory manner; but the social services department which serves as a model for policy planning and management is likely to be as rare. The 1985 SSI report said that: "A few authorities had proceeded to examine the implications of [their child care] policy for staff working in [residential] homes .... Elsewhere there was an absence of positive direction" (3). It went on: "It was apparent from the inconsistencies in standards and practice, and the defects noted, that few of the authorities had yet developed comprehensive systems for monitoring their own community homes".

4.4 An analysis of social services departments' responses to the Department's Circular LAC(91)10, which asked local authorities to examine their practices in a number of areas in the light of the "Pindown Experience" Report, showed that although some local authorities had identified good or satisfactory work being done, care practices and monitoring arrangements in a significant number of local authorities required review; and there was a general concern with the need to improve guidance to management and care staff.

4.5 The analysis of SSI reports conducted for this review called attention to the considerable pressures on the managers of individual homes. Particular issues which emerged were the importance of clearly differentiating management of the home and management of the service to the child; unrealistic expectations of first line managers; and the need for a balance to be found between staff groups which were "too stable" and those which were insufficiently so. Line management above the level of individual homes followed a number of different organisational models, and was seen as "a recipe for confused leadership and uncertainty" with a risk that homes would operate "individualistically unless respective roles and responsibilities were well-defined. They often seem not to be".

4.6 Overall it seems that there is a spectrum of social services department management styles, with considerable variations in the existence and validity of child care policies and in the effectiveness of management structures. There are undoubtedly social services departments which are efficiently run, with positive leadership,and with clearly articulated child care policies. But there are others which are weaker in all these areas. In this chapter I address, first, the adequacy of social services departments' child care policies; and, secondly, the management structures which I consider should be in place in all such departments.

CHILD CARE POLICY

4.7 On the existence and scope of child care policies in social services departments, a review of the research is revealing. A recurring theme in commentaries on the development of residential care for children in the 1980s has been the lack of a coherent policy framework for these services. As a result some staff have become isolated and demoralized, and the management of some homes idiosyncratic:

> " - the SSI report drew attention to the lack of policy guidance issued by the Council and the need for a 'sense of direction and strategy'. The expectations of residential care were found to be unclear and there was no written policy on the functions of individual children's homes, which were found to be isolated" (28).

4.8 In 1988, following the issue by SSI of a questionnaire to all English local authorities seeking information about written policies on child care, 67 sent in documents which could broadly be described as policy or strategy statements relating to work with children and families. The results of this survey showed " - a steady trend in the development of documents of this kind, and professional support for 'putting it in writing'" (20). But only a minority of documents dealt in detail with the issue of how residential care was to fit in with the overall, local strategy for child care, although more than half mentioned it as an issue. Some of the documents were brief outlines of policy, but a few were more detailed, revealing a new, strategic approach to residential care: (smaller homes, with higher staff/child ratios; staff training in new specialisms; redeployment of resources released by the closure of large, old buildings into service innovations; revision of administrative procedures). Many others covered issues of training, supervision and planning in relation to work with children in general.

4.9 The SSI report of the policy survey made the point that it was, of course, impossible to say from documents alone how far the policies which were outlined in them were having any impact on practice (though "crisis" inspections by SSI suggest the gap is wide). The review of relevant research published by the DHSS in 1985 - the "Pink Book" - found that "policies - as distinct from procedures - appear to be little known by field social workers." (29). And the recent volume, Patterns and Outcomes in Child Placement (10), commented that:

> "The... study disclosed extensive confusion among social workers about departmental policy. A typical comment (this time on rehabilitation) was: 'Existence of county policy is disputed. Fifteen respondents think there is one; fourteen do not; nine do not know.'"

4.10 Another very recent example of how difficult this is was provided by an Inspector who found that although a local authority had reported the existence of detailed policies and procedures in relation to complaints, a visit to an individual home revealed that the staff were unaware of them (communication to the Review.)

4.11 Finally, there is the question of how far guidance issued by the Department actually impinges on what social workers do. Again, the evidence suggests that even key texts, like the DHSS Code of Practice on Access, may be diluted or completely lost as it filters through local systems to the field; (see, for example Millham et al. (30)).

4.12 The message which comes through clearly from all the material referred to above is that in many departments there is a lack of clarity and comprehensiveness in implementing child care policies. These deficiencies are even more apparent in relation to residential care than other areas of children's services. The absence of a context within which to work is a strong demotivating factor for the work force; and questions whether many social services departments have a view of the purpose and direction of the services they provide. Accordingly I recommend that Directors of Social Services should verify that their arrangements for managing residential child care within an overall strategy for children's services are effective. I expand on this in the following paragraphs.

CHILD CARE PLANS

4.13   The legislation already requires:

- –   statements of purpose and care ethos for each home;
- –   published information on all children's services;
- –   individual care plans for each child being looked after.

4.14   These are important innovations. They will make explicit, in a monitorable form, the objectives of each home and the arrangements for each child. And they will give the public certain information on each authority's services for children.

4.15   I am glad to see from the Citizen's Charter that the general information on services will also say how soon individuals can expect responses to their requests for help; and that individual care plans are to include the names of the officers responsible for overseeing them.

4.16   For the statements of purpose for homes to be meaningful they must be framed in terms of an overall policy for residential child care which is not freestanding but forms part of a wider policy covering the whole range of child care policies and services. As the Children Act Guidance states:

> "Residential care remains a vital resource, but it is essential to see it as part of the overall network of services for children, used in a planned way and when it is in the best interests of the individual child. The major principles underlying the Children Act about partnership with parents, involvement of children and those with parental responsibility in decision making, proper planning and review, the right to make representations and so on, apply equally to children in residential settings and should help to ensure that their placement there is not seen in isolation from overall services to provide support to families and to children in need."

4.17   To give effect to this Guidance, local authorities will need to draw up strategies for the provision of children's services, which would state explicitly the role of residential care within the strategy. In doing so it is essential that local authorities plan their provision of community homes, taking account too of voluntary and private sector provision, in such a way as to give fullest effect to their strategies. It follows that a great deal of thought and effort will need to be put into the production of these plans and strategies. I therefore conclude that a requirement similar to a direction under Section 46(1) of the NHS and Community Care Act 1990 should be laid upon local authorities in respect of their duty to prepare and publish plans for their children's services; and that the Department of Health should issue guidance on the content of plans, and monitor their implementation.

4.18   I recommend that in monitoring the implementation of the Act, the Department should pay special attention to this area. The SSI should periodically check that all authorities have such overall plans for their children's services; that those plans are reasonably comprehensive; that they meet the purpose stated in the Guidance; and that they properly reflect the role and contributions of other agencies such as education departments, health authorities and the police.

4.19   These plans may often form the core of the information on children's services which the Act requires all local authorities to publish, though they may often be more detailed. Their monitoring by the SSI is likely to make an important contribution to the more general periodic reports on the implementation of the Act which I recommend in a later chapter that the Secretary of State should consider publishing (see paragraph 6.3).

MANAGEMENT STRUCTURES

4.20   However carefully drawn up, child care plans are only as good as the mechanism by which they are implemented. The material quoted earlier in this chapter revealed a range of problems about management structures.

4.21 The DH publication "Implementing Community Care: Purchaser, Commissioner and Provider Roles" (31) usefully sets out the aims of a mechanism for delivering policy objectives, among them:

- to clarify social services departments' goals and objectives;
- to ensure planning and budget setting are driven by the needs of the population;
- to improve the quality of services through explicitness about standards;
- to secure clear specifications of the services to be provided and costs (including unit costs);
- to improve monitoring and review in terms of quality of service and outcomes for clients;
- to facilitate increased client choice through the empowerment of care managers;
- to facilitate the identification of gaps between assessed need and available services, to be fed back into planning; and
- to secure improved value for money.

4.22 Although linked expressly to the separation of the purchaser/ commissioner and provider roles, these aims are equally valid for any management mechanism. For their achievement social services departments will need to develop, if they do not have them already, detailed information systems which enable unit costs of provision and therefore costed packages of care to be calculated. It is important that the information collected is sufficient - but no more - to inform management decisions and to enable performance to be monitored. There is some way to go before outcome measurement in child care services can be appliedgenerally; but in the meantime assessment of outputs against inputs offers a reasonable guide to performance.

4.23 I do not think that these general principles require any one form of organisation to be preferred to any other. But there needs to be consistency in the application of standards and flexibility in the approach adopted. Procedures for establishing standards need to be drawn up. Quality assurance methods should be applied throughout - above all there should be clear definitions of roles and the relationship between them to avoid duplication or omission; and good information systems to make sure that quality in service provision is maximised.

4.24 In my view this approach implies - but does not require - maximum delegation of management responsibility, including budgetary responsibility, down the line. Managing even a small home is a complex process. It requires skill and experience in working with residents individually and in groups; professional leadership and management of the staff group and management of material resources, primarily buildings and money. The job is made more difficult if elements such as resource management are removed. I conclude therefore that all heads of home should be responsible for managing all the resources of the home, and should be equipped to do so by appropriate training, experience and supervision. The head of home should be professionally qualified - see paragraph 5.12 below - but there is scope for people with qualifications in other disciplines to be appointed, provided they have appropriate experience and training.

4.25 None of this management approach is new, and local authorities are already developing information strategies and management structures along these lines in relation to community care. The separation of the purchaser/commissioner and provider roles will highlight the value of this approach by laying emphasis on unit costs of provision and standards of care. I can see no objection to this organisational model being applied to services for children, so long as the purchasers operate as if they were buying services for their own children and monitor the product in that vein. Accordingly I recommend that social services departments extend to children's services generally, and to residential child care services in particular, the management principles and techniques referred to above; and that the Department of Health issue guidance to local authorities to assist in this process. I commend the admirable Children Act Guidance on all aspects of staffing.

ROLES OF SOCIAL SERVICES COMMITTEE MEMBERS

4.26 Having considered the process of policy formulation and the management structures by which they should be implemented I next consider the roles of SSC members. Both the "Pindown Experience" Report (Conclusion (xxvi), page 169) and the earlier Report "A Child in Trust" (32) commented on failures by elected members in discharging their responsibilities towards children in the Council's care.

4.27 Councillors are responsible to the electorate in respect of all the statutory duties imposed on their authority, although the manner in which they are performed depends to some degree upon the nature of the statutory duty. Members of Social Services Committees should not be concerned solely with managing the authority's services and the prudent husbandry of its resources: they are responsible also for discharging the Council's role as good parent towards the children in its care. It is significant to note the detail in which local authority responsibilities are spelled out in statute, regulations and guidance, which exceed any statements in law of the responsibilities of natural parents. This reflects "a higher duty than that of the reasonable parent" (to quote Louis Blom-Cooper QC in "A Child in Trust") upon the local authority where the care of the child depends upon a public, corporate parent.

4.28 Members currently discharge these responsibilities in a variety of ways. Rota visiting is common and Regulation 22 of the Children's Homes Regulations 1991 refers to this function for Members who wish to perform it. Some authorities delegate to officers all responsibility other than that expressly reserved to Members. Others involve Members in the detail of day to day business.

4.29 I have no sense of a common pattern to the role of Members in discharging an authority's parenting responsibilities. I have seen the useful guide for local authority councillors produced by the University of Leicester (33). I have also seen parts of a draft guide for elected Members on Social Services Committees by Mr J M Richards, which addresses some of these issues. I conclude that further work is called for to establish models of practice for Members in discharging the parental responsibilities of local authorities towards the children they look after. I recommend that this be commissioned by the Local Authority Associations.

REGULATORY INSPECTION

4.30 Inspection is a method or process which may have a number of purposes. I use the term regulatory inspection to denote the type of scrutiny which checks adherence to statute, regulations and guidance. It is most effective in scrutinising processes which are readily observable and measurable. Inspection linked to the assessment of outcome, quality and standards ("developmental inspection") requires a more sophisticated approach. Regulatory inspection has the largely protective function of ensuring that the basic requirements of a service are complied with. Developmental inspection has the function of providing the empirical evidence against which progress in policy and practice can be monitored, and is the method now largely employed by SSI in its selective programme of inspection.

4.31 Regulatory inspection protects by providing a snapshot of services at a particular point in time. Its viewpoint is independent of management. It gives a reasonable basis for broad assumptions about the ethos and culture of an institution, but cannot convey complete confidence either that everything has been disclosed or that incidents of poor practice will not occur tomorrow.

4.32 Inspection is itself a resource-intensive activity, requiring investment in planning and in reporting back as well as on site visits. The latter, moreover, must be thorough if they are to be effective: two Inspectors are needed except for the smallest homes, and an overnight stay is essential to observing and understanding the life of the establishment. There must be a trade-off between the resources needed for inspection and those needed for providing the service. My view is that regulatory inspection less frequently than one substantial and one follow-up inspection each year is likely to be only marginally effective. The protective element is likely to be enhanced, and the developmental element reduced, by unheralded visits.

4.33   Neither form of inspection is in any sense a substitute for the responsible discharge of all the responsibilities of management. Both can assist management, applied separately or combined, by a dispassionate external scrutiny of the service (and, in the case of developmental work, by assisting in the preparation of future plans drawn up in accordance with national policies and standards). Neither can compensate for deficiencies of management: both provide additional safeguards for people living in residential homes; the best safeguard remains the commitment and competence of the body responsible for and the people running the home.

INSPECTION AND THE CHILDREN ACT

4.34   Private children's homes will be registered by local authorities when the Children Act (Section 63) comes into force on 14 October 1991. Registration must be reviewed annually. Regulation 28 of the Children's Homes Regulations 1991 requires local authorities to cause registered children's homes to be inspected at least twice each year.

4.35   Voluntary homes continue to be registered by the Secretary of State by virtue of Section 60 of the Act. They are inspected by the Social Services Inspectorate on behalf of the Secretary of State. The Inspectorate's current practice is to inspect homes run by the three largest voluntary agencies every three years and other homes annually.

4.36   Community homes lack any system of external regulatory inspection other than in respect of secure accommodation in community homes, which must be approved annually by the Secretary of State and is inspected by SSI for that purpose. But the Secretary of State has general powers of inspection (which are extended by Section 80 of the Act to any premises to which the Act applies in which a child is accommodated), which may be formally invoked in certain circumstances.

4.37   This position is unsatisfactory on two counts. All local authority residential homes except community homes are now subject to systematic inspection. Moreover, there is little to suggest that community homes differ sufficiently from independent children's homes to justify a different approach to inspection. For these reasons I consider that all community homes including controlled and assisted homes should in future be formally and regularly inspected.

4.38   Who should inspect community homes? The local authority will register and inspect private children's homes; the Inspectorate inspects secure accommodation in community homes and voluntary homes. These seem to be the only candidates; establishing an ad hoc third force for residential child care, detached from responsibilities for policy, services and resources, is impracticable.

4.39   It has been put to me in the course of the review that children's services are a special case by virtue of the vulnerability of that age group, that central Government has direct responsibilities for protecting children and particular responsibility for ensuring that the intentions of Parliament as expressed in the Children Act are complied with, and that SSI should therefore assume the systematic inspection of community homes as well as voluntary homes.

4.40   I find it difficult to sustain a case for regarding any one category of residential user as more vulnerable than another. Moreover I note that Volume 4 of The Children Act Guidance makes it plain at paragraph 1.15 that "Inspections should normally be carried out by the Social Services Department's Independent Inspection Unit". I note, too, the policy decision that so far as possible local services should be inspected locally; and that residential homes for disabled children are inspected by local authority inspection units.

4.41 I conclude therefore that inspection of community homes should be undertaken by the independent inspection units established in local authorities, as is already suggested in the Children Act Guidance. But while that Guidance is a significant move in the right direction I consider that to bring such homes fully into line with other local authority homes the Secretary of State should issue a direction requiring them to be subject to arm's length inspection. It follows that it would be anomalous for individual voluntary homes to continue to be registered by the Secretary of State; accordingly I recommend that these homes should also come within the remit of the local authority's inspection units and be subject to the same frequency of inspection as for other homes. It should be a condition of this new arrangement that the inspection units should include staff experienced in work with children, and in the management of residential homes. Some should have experience in independent agencies.

4.42 Arrangements for approving secure accommodation, however, should remain with the Secretary of State, since arrangements affecting the liberty of the citizen are properly for central Government, and the associated inspection is properly undertaken by SSI.

4.43 Monitoring the implementation of the whole of the Children Act and associated guidance is plainly the duty of the Department of Health, but it would be proper for the Secretary of State to require inspection units to monitor the extent to which practice reflects the relevant Regulations and Guidance as part of their regulatory functions.

4.44 Earlier Departmental guidance (Chapter 5 of "Community Care in the Next Decade and Beyond") usefully sets out the basic constitution and functions of inspection units. The additional advice promised by the Department of Health about the application of these units to children's services should take account of any special features of the local authority's responsibility towards children: in particular, its direct, parental responsibilities towards children in care. The work of the unit in this area should be reported to the Social Services Committee more frequently than annually (the intervals to be determined in accordance with local policies) and should among other things assess how far residential services for children accord with the Children Act Regulations and Guidance.

4.45 Existing guidance puts inspection units on a line reporting to the Director of Social Services, who is as the chief officer ultimately accountable for any deficiencies in management the units detect. Given the responsibilities of local authorities towards children in care, I expect the head of the unit to be able to report directly to the Director on matters concerning children's services. The Inspectorate has work in hand on inspection procedures. That work should ensure that the inspection process is properly subject to monitoring by independent interests external to the authority and representatives of the users themselves.

4.46 In relation to these units SSI should, as set out in the guidance, continue to "monitor the progress of inspection units from April 1991. In particular, the Inspectorate will examine the operational framework of the unit and its role and functions within the SSD; the links between the unit and other agencies; recruitment practices; the consultative arrangements; the working methods and standards applied and the follow-up arrangements made. The Inspectorate will also seek to measure the adequacy of the response made by authorities to reports on their own homes."

4.47 The Inspectorate has already published its Guidance on Practice for Inspection Units "Inspecting for Quality" (28). Two volumes of its Guidance on Standards for Residential Homes have also appeared; it should issue the companion volume on Residential Homes for Children as soon as possible.

SECURE ACCOMMODATION

4.48 Secure accommodation is a necessary part of the residential child care system, because it enables children to be protected from suffering significant harm or injuring themselves or others. I have considered the safeguards applying to the use of secure accommodation under existing legislation, and the improvements which will be introduced once the Children Act and the Children (Secure Accommodation) Regulations 1991 come into operation. These are important provisions, as the restricting of liberty deprives a person of a fundamental right. So it is essential that in relation to children the safeguards are sufficient and satisfactory.

4.49   Sometimes the line between control of a child's behaviour and the restriction of his or her liberty is finely drawn. The Pindown approach clearly incorporated the deliberate - and illegal - restriction of liberty. Practices where children are confined to locked rooms, sometimes referred to as "time out", are equally culpable. If there is doubt whether a practice infringes the child's right of liberty legal advice should be sought. This is clearly expressed in Volume 4 of the Children Act Guidance, and I welcome it. Placement in secure accommodation should never be used as a form of punishment.

4.50   Where secure accommodation in a community home has been approved by the Secretary of State, there must be a risk that its availability tempts staff to use it where the deprivation of a child's liberty is not essential, or to keep a child in it longer than is strictly necessary. In either case the restriction of liberty would be unjustifiable. The statutory safeguards available for children in such situations should, however, prove effective. The duty on local authorities, introduced by the Act, to take reasonable steps to avoid children being placed in secure accommodation will provide further useful protection. So too will the general requirement for a guardian ad litem to be appointed in court proceedings considering placement of a child in secure accommodation.

4.51   The Secretary of State has to approve all facilities in community homes which are intended for use as secure accommodation. But at present there is no requirement for him to approve secure accommodation in other settings. As children being looked after by local authorities may be placed in residential care other than in children's homes, for example in NHS establishments, there is a gap in the existing legislation. This gap will not be filled by the Children Act. I conclude accordingly that all secure accommodation in health care premises, whether NHS or private - or indeed in educational settings - should be approved by the Secretary of State before it is used for accommodating children.

4.52   A more significant gap has existed, however, in the availability of safeguards governing the restriction of liberty of children accommodated outside local authority community homes. I note and welcome the fact that the Children Act will close this gap by extending the safeguards applying in community homes to children placed in health or local education authority accommodation. From October this year a health or local education authority will need to apply to a court for permission to place (or keep) a child in secure accommodation. The same statutory protection will also apply to children accommodated in residential care homes, nursing homes and mental nursing homes.

4.53   It is important to consider whether those classes of children who will not benefit from the safeguards in Section 25 of the Children Act are reasonably excluded. In my view it is right that children who, having committed serious offences, have been sentenced under Section 53 of the Children and Young Persons Act 1933 should be excluded. The nature of their offences takes them into the well established procedures of the criminal justice system where deprivation of liberty is the expected sanction.

4.54   Another class of excluded children is those detained under the Mental Health Act 1983, and adequate safeguards are available for them under that Act in respect of the use of secure accommodation. Finally, children over 16 to whom Section 20(5) of the Children Act applies, and those in respect of whom there is a child assessment order where the child is kept away from home, are also excluded on the grounds that they should never be locked up - a policy which I fully support.

4.55   On more general matters, I note that it is the policy of the Department of Health to encourage the more rational, effective and efficient use of existing secure accommodation in community homes, and to promote - through greater co-operation between local authorities - a more even geographical spread on a regional basis. These seem to be laudable objectives, which I support.

4.56   Their importance is given added weight by the Home Office proposal to end the practice of remanding juvenile boys into custody. I believe this is the right policy direction. But if an adequate range of suitable provision within the community is to be available to such children, it will be necessary to increase the number of secure places overall, and ensure that their distribution around the country is adequate. Nevertheless I very much hope that it will prove possible to examine closely the options for caring for these remanded young people safely without recourse in every case to secure accommodation. I note that a national task group has now been established by the Department, involving local authority and other interests, to draw up a strategy for reaching this goal. This will clearly need to give careful consideration to the resource implications.

THE INTERFACE WITH OTHER RESIDENTIAL CHILD CARE PROVISION

4.57   The Children Act, together with its associated regulations, make radically new arrangements for the protection of children's interests in residential homes. But the range of such homes is wide and the bodies responsible for them diverse. In particular I believe that the treatment and detention of children in psychiatric settings raise complex issues which are beyond the scope of this review. Accordingly I consider that the Government should now check that the regulatory procedures affecting children in residential placements other than in children's homes are suitable, and imply the same standards of protection where that would be justified.

CHAPTER 5

RESOURCES

INTRODUCTION

5.1   This chapter considers the various resources available for the provision of residential child care. It looks first at staffing, including pay, conditions of service and training; then at the accommodation used for these services; and finally the overall level of funding.

STAFFING

5.2   Regulation 5(1) of the Children's Homes Regulations 1991 will require the responsible authority to ensure "that the number of staff of each children's home and their experience and qualifications are adequate to ensure that the welfare of the children accommodated there is safeguarded and promoted at all times". This is helpfully developed in the associated Guidance.

5.3   In September 1989, 10,800 care staff (whole time equivalents) were employed in local authority community homes. The ratio of care staff to residents had improved from 1:1.8 to 1:1 in 10 years. This increased ratio is a welcome and necessary response to the changing nature of residential care in looking after children presenting a greater concentration of challenging behaviour and complex problems than hitherto. Other factors are significant in this respect, such as qualifications, training and staff turnover.

5.4   Particularly important is the matching of staff to the functions performed in residential child care. What those functions are depends on the purpose and the size of the particular home. Common to all are those aims and objectives which give effect to the central purposes of residential child care described in Chapter 2 of Part 2 of this Report. It follows that social work is the core discipline in residential child care. Residential care is, and should be seen to be, a part of social work generally - not as something different in kind from community-based social work. There should be movement and career progression (in both directions) between social work in community and in residential settings. Social workers should be encouraged and enabled to move more easily than at present between the two for career experience and development.

5.5   Although social work is the core discipline, the functions of direct personal care and management are equally important. The way these functions are combined in a home determines its characteristic culture and ethos, and affect the nature of its relationships with other bodies as well as with the local community. For staff these functions combine in different ways depending on the individual's role within the home. I have already emphasised in Chapter 4 of Part 2 the importance of defining roles to avoid gaps or overlaps in functions.

QUALIFICATIONS

5.6   How should staff be matched with roles which reflect these different elements? Management must define the level of qualification and training required for each role, and draw up and implement personnel management policies to achieve them. I commissioned a survey to find out the present state of qualification and experience among residential staff. Twenty local authorities were asked to complete a questionnaire, and all responded most helpfully. The exercise was carefully designed to ensure that the findings would be representative of the national picture.

5.7   I note in passing that statistics on the qualifications and training of the social services workforce are not collected as a matter of routine. I fail to see how plans can be made for personnel planning and management without such information. I conclude that the Department of Health and the Local Authority Associations should consider what statistics should in future be collected.

5.8   The evidence from the survey, summarised in Appendix 6, was not encouraging. Of all officers in charge 33 per cent held a Certificate of Qualification in Social Work (CQSW); 40 per cent held a Certificate in Social Service (CSS); and 6 per cent a social care qualification. The remaining 20 per cent had no qualifications. Fewer than 50 per cent of assistant officers in charge had a social work or social care qualification. 37 per cent had been in post for under two years.

5.9   No more than five per cent of care staff held either the CQSW or CSS, and a further 18 per cent held another social care qualification - leaving over 75 per cent with no qualifications. 45 per cent of care staff had been in post for under 2 years.

5.10   Overall the survey showed that the vast majority - 70 per cent - of staff of local authority homes for children were unqualified, and with a significant number being unqualified and in post for under 2 years. Such information as exists suggests that the proportion of residential child care staff who possess a relevant qualification is no higher than it was ten years ago, which would mean in fact a net loss of trained staff from residential care.

5.11   The general picture is exemplified by the 'Analysis of Thirty SSI Inspection Reports' between 1987 and 1991 conducted for the review which confirmed that officers in charge generally held a professional qualification but few if any other staff members were qualified except in large complex establishments employing those qualified in other fields (such as teachers, nurses and psychologists).

5.12   This situation is deplorable. Leadership and oversight is needed in every home by someone who is suitably qualified. The functions of residential care set out in paragraph 5.5 above call for a thorough knowledge of the principles and methods of social work. There needs to be leadership and oversight in every home by someone who is suitably qualified in this area. I conclude that local authorities should as a matter of priority draw up plans whereby, as a first step, all officers in charge not holding the CQSW or CSS should obtain the appropriate minimum qualification - now the Diploma in Social Work (DipSW) - although holders of other full, relevant professional qualifications might be excepted. As the DipSW qualifying period is 2 years, I consider it would be reasonable for local authorities to achieve this objective within 3 years.

5.13   The functions of residential child care set out in this report suggest that about one third of the care staff overall might need the DipSW or a relevant professional equivalent if they are to be effectively performed. The balance between staff with different qualifications is ultimately for individual employers to decide. The overall balance needs more detailed scrutiny, and I suggest that the Joint Inquiry consider the matter further.

5.14 The introduction of National Vocational Qualifications (NVQ) provides a structure within which unqualified staff can, by demonstrating competence in specific areas, obtain different levels of qualification. These levels have been aligned to allow staff to progress up to, and including, the DipSW qualification. I add to that one further important point: that managers should set for staff who are yet to reach the first level of NVQ clear objectives for personal development, for attainment within specific timetables. This is important in personnel management terms, and desirable in preparing staff for progression through NVQ to DipSW standard.

5.15   Management should not regard attainment of the DipSW as marking the end of the qualifications path. The availability and coverage of post-qualifying training is being increased, and the elements which relate directly to residential child care are being significantly expanded. There will, therefore, be many more opportunities in future for DipSW holders to develop their knowledge and skills, and they should do so.

5.16   I have not considered in detail the scope and content of NVQ, the DipSW and post-qualifying training. But I have received evidence, which I find persuasive, that the range of NVQ competences which relate to residential care is too narrow. In particular I can see advantage in including both child protection and control techniques within NVQ. In relation to the DipSW I believe that there is scope not only for laying greater emphasis on the residential care element (including the work experience placement) but also on the principles and practice of management. I do not share the view that training in management should follow qualifying training. The importance I place on management skills derives from my conclusions in the previous chapter, which I believe argue forcefully for the inclusion of the essentials of management in qualifying training.

5.17 I am conscious of the large practical and resource difficulties in increasing the quantity and take-up of qualifying and post-qualifying courses. The cumulative cost of developing qualifying training to the level required for even one third of residential child care staff is likely to be over £30 million, divided between individual local authorities and the Department of Health. The practical problems of expanding training courses are also formidable. Such considerations do not in themselves justify dismissing my proposals as unrealistic. And the risks of perpetuating the use of undertrained and inexperienced staff in this important and exacting sector of work are immense. I consider that the Department of Health, the Local Authorities Associations and CCETSW should formulate an action plan, within the strategy for social services training, for securing the number of qualified staff needed within 5 years. They should also appoint an expert group to report, within 6 months, on the residential child care content of qualifying courses.

TRAINING

5.18 The record of residential care staff with regard to training is much more comforting than for qualifications, and has been given fresh impetus by the introduction in 1989 of the Training Support Programme (Child Care). In its first year 7,600 residential care staff received general child care training, and 4,300 received child protection training. In 1990/91 over 6,000 residential care staff were expected to receive general child care training, 7,000 child protection training, and 11,000 introductory training about the Children Act. While this record of performance is entirely laudable, there is scope for re-emphasising within the 1992-93 programme the priority given to the specific training needs of residential care staff, and I recommend that the Department of Health should do so. I also recommend that the Department of Health should give priority, in discharging the Secretary of State's duty under Section 83 of the Act, to review the adequacy of child care training.

PERSONNEL MANAGEMENT

5.19 Getting the system of qualifications and training right is only one part of the solution to the widespread problems of low morale and status within residential child care. Residential care is used by some people as a useful route into social work; as soon as they obtain their social work qualification they move out into community-based work where morale and status are higher. I have considered what needs to be done to retain a higher proportion in residential care and also encourage movement in the other direction. I conclude that much can be done under the general heading of personnel management.

5.20 The survey of qualifications among residential staff also recorded time spent in the post held. From this came evidence of polarisation between a significant number of staff who had been in post a short time and those who had been in post for considerably longer. This picture fits with general impressions gained from SSI inspections of a core of residential care stalwarts who have not had, and do not desire, experience in other fields of social work. It supports the notion of residential care being used by a number of other staff as a springboard for social work generally.

5.21 What this points to is the need for a more managerially-led staffing policy throughout child care services generally. Such a policy would be based on the expectation that a career in social work would require experience of both residential and community-based social work. Career progression would, as now, be linked to the attainment of qualifications and post-qualifying credits. There would, however, need to be in future some recognition of the value of practical experience, expressed in the form of standard "postings" lasting for specified periods in certain areas. Such an approach would powerfully assist the integration of residential care within social work generally; and, by establishing expectations about length of stay in post, help to counter the drainage of qualified staff into fieldwork. It should also provide incentives for qualified field workers to cross into residential care management.

5.22 A positively-led personnel management policy would also encourage those whose ambitions do not extend beyond residential care to acquire a broader perspective of social work generally, and the role of residential care within it. This is important in countering the tendency in some homes towards insularity and inwardness, which is so often the breeding ground of unprofessional practices. It should also help in promoting a greater awareness of the roles of individual postholders within the tauter management structures which I advocate in Chapter 4 of Part 2.

5.23 Considerable thought needs to be given to the way in which positive personnel management policies of this kind should be implemented. In many social services departments something of this kind is already in place; in others the baseline is much lower. I conclude therefore that the Local Authorities Associations (or the Local Government Management Board on their behalf) should draw up guidance in this area for social services departments within 6 months.

5.24 Staff need to be assured that what they are doing is valued, important and will endure. That assurance is primarily for the employers, and senior managers in the organisations which require and provide residential care, to give. I trust that employers and the Joint Inquiry will address this issue. In support of this new approach I consider that the professional social work associations should demonstrate their leadership by evolving and implementing policies for restoring the high status of residential child care which was previously established by such a champion as Lyward. In doing so I see scope for building on the attractiveness of residential care for those who wish to combine management responsibility with continuing contact with clients.

CONDITIONS OF SERVICE

5.25 As part of a personnel management policy it will be necessary to review the conditions of service in residential homes. A conventional working week has little reality in residential care, and stereotyped systems of shift-working do not suit the task because they take insufficient account of the best interests of children. Applying the test of the "good parent" leads to the conclusion that a change in conditions is needed. Continuity in the caring roles for the home's residents suggests a return to appropriately adapted patterns of living-in staff, and I have received representations seeking a return to just such an arrangement. I have much sympathy with this because young people are unlikely to place much value on the establishment they live in if all the staff choose to live elsewhere. The home secures a clearer identity if a member of staff actually lives there. I hope that the Joint Inquiry will consider these matters further.

PAY

5.26 Simply increasing rates of pay for residential care staff would neither solve the problems of status and morale nor be an effective use of resources. If other elements are right the issue of pay becomes less crucial. Basic salaries should be fixed according to qualification, with incremental progress for experience and satisfactory performance. Changes in salary levels should be linked directly with change in job content, performance or the level of qualification held; and with the characteristics of residential care that distinguish it from social work in other settings. I suggest that the Joint Inquiry should start from this position.

BUILDINGS USED FOR PROVIDING RESIDENTIAL CARE

5.27   There are about 1,000 local authority community homes, 81 voluntary homes and around 100 registered children's homes in England. Little is known about their physical state or the facilities they provide. What data we have is subjective, often impressionistic and not systematic.

5.28   A survey of 30 SSI reports on children's homes reveals considerable variation in their condition, some displaying good physical standards whilst others show signs of neglect and even decay. Within the limits of the data one may reasonably conclude that purpose-built establishments are, as a class, no better or worse than adapted premises. Although the latter are generally older, they have a character which contributes positively to the ambience of the home.

5.29   The Children Act Guidance contains much useful detail about the nature, layout and facilities of residential homes which should apply to adapted as well as to purpose-built premises. I commend this Guidance. The creation of a pleasant, homely environment, with the emphasis on privacy, independence and choice, has an important influence on children's attitudes to care. It also affects staff morale, and helps to shape the local community's reactions to the children and staff.

5.30   I confine my comments on local authorities' building stock to two points. First, that the quality of care provided in a home is related to the design and attractiveness of the home; it is important for it to be well laid out, suitably equipped, properly maintained and attractively decorated. Secondly, that there is considerable advantage, again in terms of quality of care, for keeping the home fairly small. Research by Martin Knapp at the University of Kent at Canterbury (34) suggests an optimal size of 14 children for efficient use of resources; others persuaded by primarily professional considerations have recommended a figure of 8. There are already good examples of children cared for in groups of 4 or 5 in "ordinary" homes staffed by residential social workers. It would be sensible for local authorities to plan their homes stock on the basis of a capacity which lies in this range.

RESOURCING OF RESIDENTIAL CHILD CARE

5.31   How much money is spent on residential care is a matter for the local authority: in the context of how much it spends on children's services generally, on social services overall, and ultimately on all the services for which it is responsible. How much money it is able to spend in all depends to some considerable extent on decisions by central government about the size of its financial contribution to local services and the methods by which it is distributed.

5.32   The conventions governing the relationships between central and local Government on financial matters preclude the Secretary of State from determining or directing local authority spending on residential child care as a whole.

5.33   During the past decade gross spending by local authorities in England on personal social services has risen by 25 per cent at constant prices*, from £3.4 billion in 1979-80 to £4.2 billion in 1989-90. Over the same period the gross amount spent on children's services has also risen, from £0.74 billion to £0.75 billion - an increase of 2 per cent at constant prices.

5.34   That 2 per cent increase represents a combination of two very different trends. Spending on residential child care fell at constant prices by 36 per cent over the decade, whereas expenditure on other services for children rose by 100 per cent. In respect of children local authorities spent more in 1989-90 on non-residential services than on residential care; by contrast, in 1979-80 the cost of residential child care services was two and a half times that of non-residential children's services.

*1989-90 personal social services pay and prices

5.35   These trends need to be viewed against changes in demography over the decade. Between 1980 and 1990 the number of children aged 0-17 declined by 10 per cent. The number of children received into local authority care fell more sharply, by nearly 40 per cent (from 95,300 to 60,500); and for those in residential care the decline was even more marked: a decrease of nearly 65 per cent (from 37,400 to 13,200). The proportion of children in care placed in residential care has almost halved, from 39 per cent in 1980 to 22 per cent in 1990.

5.36   Although numbers of children in residential care and the cost of residential care provision in real terms have bothdeclined, the unit cost of residential provision in community homes (which represents 80 per cent of total expenditure on residential child care) has risen consistently over the past ten years. At constant prices the gross unit cost per child in community homes rose from £326 in 1979-80 to £537 per week in 1989-90 - that is, by 65 per cent. The upward trend has not been consistent, with the biggest rise occurring in the first half of the decade. This is shown in figure 6, in comparison with trends in unit costs for other client groups.

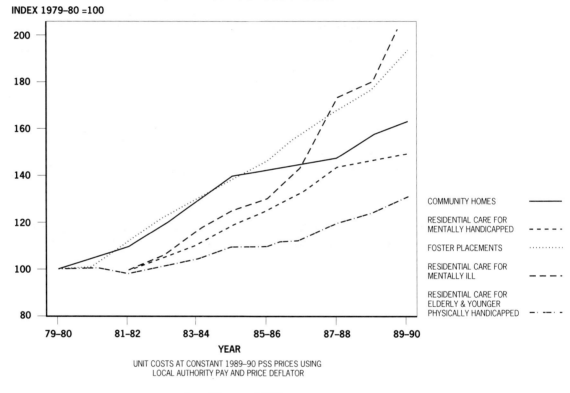

TRENDS IN UNIT COSTS BY CLIENT GROUP

INDEX 1979–80 =100

COMMUNITY HOMES

RESIDENTIAL CARE FOR MENTALLY HANDICAPPED

FOSTER PLACEMENTS

RESIDENTIAL CARE FOR MENTALLY ILL

RESIDENTIAL CARE FOR ELDERLY & YOUNGER PHYSICALLY HANDICAPPED

YEAR

UNIT COSTS AT CONSTANT 1989–90 PSS PRICES USING LOCAL AUTHORITY PAY AND PRICE DEFLATOR

figure 6 (paragraph 5.35)

5.37   This upward trend, which is consistent with the trend in unit costs of residential provision for other client groups, may be explained in a number of ways. Although throughout the decade the number of staff in residential child care fell, the rate of decline was not as fast as for the children themselves. As a proportion of overall unit costs the staffing element (including domestic and ancillary staff) increased from 61 per cent in 1979-80 to 69 per cent in 1984-85. This change was accompanied by an increase in the ratio of staff numbers per child from 0.86 to 1.28. From 1984-85 to 1988-89 the staffing element remained at about the same proportion of overall unit costs, although the staffing ratio improved further, from 1.28 to 1.40. These improvements in the staffing ratio over the past decade include the marked improvement in the ratio of care staff to children referred to in paragraph 5.3 above. (Although on the face of it such a trend might imply a comparable improvement in quality of care, a host of factors prevent such a conclusion from being drawn in such simple terms).

5.38 Because staff costs generally rise more rapidly than non-staff costs, some upward movement in the proportion of overall unit costs that they represent is to be expected. But a comparison with pay scales generally within the personal social services suggests that the cost per staff (whole time equivalent) in residential care has risen slightly more rapidly over the past ten years, with the greater increases occurring in the period from 1979-80 to 1984-85. Possible reasons for this include higher pay rises for residential staff, more overtime or other enhancements of basic pay, or changes in staff mix in residential homes.

5.39 Other factors could also significantly affect unit costs of residential provision, for example changes in occupancy levels. It seems reasonable to assume that occupancy levels will have had a bearing because, despite the rapidly declining numbers of children in residential care, local authorities would not have been able to reduce their costs of provision as fast. Until numbers of children had fallen to the point where homes could be closed local authorities would have little scope for realising savings in respect of residential care. Savings from reductions in staff have been limited by the policy of improving staff/child ratios.

FUTURE RESOURCES

5.40 The large increase in the unit cost of looking after children in residential homes during the last decade, taken with the large increase in staff/child ratios that has mainly caused it, suggest how dangerous it is to assume that the problems remaining in the residential care sector will necessarily be resolved by further cost increases. But it is inevitable that my recommendations for increasing the number of residential staff in child care who have appropriate qualifications and training will require additional resources. These, and any resource implications arising out of further work and analysis, or future developments affecting the sector, will need to be addressed constructively by local and central Government through the normal processes (described in Appendix 5). But it is already clear from my review that the main problems probably lie elsewhere - in the care policies pursued in these homes and their relationship to other child care services, the professional formation and personnel management of their staffs; and above all in the effectiveness with which authorities and their senior managers define their roles, take a progressive and proactive approach to staff management, and monitor and where necessary bring about change where this is necessary.

CHAPTER 6

THE FUTURE

THE CHILDREN ACT: REGULATIONS AND GUIDANCE

6.1   On 25 July the Government published Volume 4 of the Children Act Guidance. Volume 4 covers residential care, and although there is much new material in it, a good deal is also carried forward from other Volumes.

6.2   I have studied this new Guidance carefully. I find it impressive in its coverage, and in the depth in which it addresses the issues. It sets out in very clear terms the philosophy behind the Children Act, and how that is given effect through the various Regulations. It is a laudable document, and one which adds very considerably to the quality of existing guidance on residential child care. As such it has provided a fixed point of reference for this Review which has been invaluable in assisting me with my task. I have asked witnesses to comment to me on the Guidance and have been much heartened by the consistently warm welcome it has received from them.

IMPLEMENTATION OF THE ACT

6.3   The new Act and its associated Regulations and Guidance provide a radically improved framework for the development of all services - residential and other - for children. It is one of the most important pieces of social policy legislation of recent decades. It places on local authorities and others important and difficult responsibilities. I have no doubt that the Government will be monitoring its implementation carefully and I suggest that the Secretary of State for Health should consider making periodic public reports of progress. These reports should be informed by the SSI's and the Department's assessments of the implementation process; but should also, so far as possible, take account of views expressed by interested and informed parties outside both local and central government.

6.4   In addition I recommend that the Department Health report to the Secretary of State in 18 months' time on the first year's operation of the Children's Homes Regulations and associated Guidance; and institute such further arrangements for monitoring as then seem desirable.

RESEARCH

6.5   One of the features of the Children Act and of the associated Regulations and Guidance is the extent to which they have drawn on the outstanding research into child care of recent years. Much of this is helpfully summarised for practitioners in two Departmental publications: Social Work Decisions in Child Care (29) and Patterns and Outcomes in Child Placement (10). The changes brought about by the Children Act deserve careful evaluation. The Department of Health has planned its own programme, and I trust that other sponsors of research will ensure a suitable place for this in their own future work.

6.6   The Department has in hand or is commissioning a programme of further work:

   ★   Training - the Training Support Programme has been continued and extended; the Open University training package on working with children and young people was substantially funded by the Department; training aids will be developed for residential staff working with difficult adolescents;

   ★   Research - an important conference for senior managers and researchers will be held in the Autumn;

★ Development - a group at the National Institute for Social Work, chaired by Barbara Kahan and funded by the Department, is preparing detailed practice guidance on residential child care; and the Social Services Inspectorate will undertake a range of development work later this year aimed at stimulating positive change.

CHAPTER 7

CONCLUSIONS

AND RECOMMENDATIONS

(RECOMMENDATIONS ARE UNDERLINED)

RESIDENTIAL CARE: ROLE AND FUNCTIONS
(CHAPTERS 1 AND 2)

1. Residential Care is an indispensable service:

    that should be a positive, joint choice, primarily for adolescents, who may present challenging behaviour.

2. The purpose of residential care is to provide:

    ★ a home for children who:
    ★ have decided that they do not wish to be fostered;
    ★ have had bad experiences of foster care;
    ★ have been so abused within the family that another family placement is inappropriate;
    ★ are from the same family and cannot otherwise be kept together;
    – expert, multidisciplinary help with social and personal problems in a residential setting;
    – containment and help in conditions of security.

    Residential homes fulfil a specialist role as partners in a range of preventive and rehabilitative services designed to meet specific needs: observation and assessment, permanent family placement, juvenile justice projects, respite care for disabled children, and preparation for independent living.

3. Residents should participate in decisions affecting the life of the home, and have proper expectations of what living there should offer them.

4. The special needs of children from black and minority ethnic groups should be considered on every issue affecting the care of children.

WELFARE OF CHILDREN (CHAPTER 3)

5. Placement: discriminating match of residents to home is obligatory; a range of children living together is preferred, with specialised care available separately for those who need it, abused children not placed with abusers, contamination by serious criminal behaviour avoided.

6. Care authorities should act to

    (i) meet health needs

    Recommendations

    6.1 Individual homes to include programmes of health education and health care in their statements of objectives (paragraph 3.24).
    6.2 Care authorities secure with health authorities local agreements for providing psychological and psychiatric support for children being looked after (paragraph 3.25).
    6.3 The Department of Health consider whether a further review is needed of those services (paragraph 3.25).
    6.4 The Department of Health require health authorities to co-operate with local authorities in producing plans for children's services (paragraph 3.27).
    6.5 Care authorities invoke Section 27 of the Act in cases of difficulty in meeting the educational, health or housing needs of individual children (paragraph 3.26).

(ii)   remedy educational disadvantage

Recommendations

6.6   <u>The Department of Health discuss with the Department of Education and Science the feasibility of guidance to education authorities about the educational needs of children being looked after by local authorities (paragraph 3.27).</u>

6.7   <u>Joint education and social services sub-committees of local authorities devise and implement strategies to meet the educational needs of children in care, including those who have left school (paragraph 3.27).</u>

(iii) encourage creative leisure pursuits

Recommendation

6.8   <u>Care authorities make full use of youth and educational services in devising constructive programmes of leisure activities, and participate in programmes of crime prevention (paragraphs 3.28 and 3.44).</u>

(iv)   facilitate cultural and spiritual development

(v)   promote employment prospects

Recommendation

6.9   <u>The Review supports recommendation 13.38 of the report 'The Pindown Experience' about the appointment and responsibilities of a named senior manager, and recommends its general application (paragraph 3.33).</u>

vi)   prepare residents for independent living

(vii) and co-ordinate after care.

Recommendation

6.10 <u>Care authorities include health, education, leisure, employment and after care in their care plans for individual children (paragraph 3.33).</u>

7.   Residential care has a key role in protecting children.

Management must be alert to the risk of abuse by staff, but support appropriate physical contact with residents.

Disabled children are particularly vulnerable.

Recommendations

7.1   <u>In the light of the operation of the new complaints procedure, the Department of Health consider extending the role of the Independent Visitor, particularly in relation to children with disabilities, but also in relation to all children in residential care (paragraphs 3.39 and 3.48).</u>

7.2   <u>The Local Authority Associations consider offering the service of independent adjudication in cases of intractable dispute between a child and the care authority (paragraph 3.50).</u>

8.   Staff are insufficiently trained in how to maintain a controlled environment; training is important in managing situations of potential violence.

Recommendation

8.1   <u>Department of Health consider with other groups or individuals, notably the Central Council for Education and Training in Social Work, guidance on the content of in-service training on constructive methods of control (paragraph 3.59).</u>

MANAGEMENT (CHAPTER 4)

9. All social services departments need statements of their policies for child care, which should be the foundations for the planning, management and review of their child care services, including residential care.

Recommendation

9.1 The Secretary of State issue a direction requiring local authorities to produce and publish plans for children's services; the Department of Health to issue guidance on the content of plans and monitor their implementation (paragraph 4.17).

10. Residential care presents difficulties of management and supervision to which social services departments respond with a spectrum of management styles of variable effectiveness.

Recommendation

10.1 Directors of Social Services verify that arrangements for managing residential child care within an overall strategy for children's services are effective (paragraph 4.12).

11. There is a lack of clarity and comprehensiveness in implementing policy.

Recommendations

11.1 Social services departments extend to children's services, including residential care, management principles and techniques concerning information systems, standard setting and quality assurance; and the Department of Health issue guidance (paragraph 4.25).

11.2 The local authority associations commission or undertake guidance on the role of local authority members in relation to children being looked after by the authority (paragraph 4.29).

12. The head of home is a key figure in establishing the culture, ethos and professional practice of the home.

Recommendation

12.1 Heads of homes manage all the resources of the home (paragraph 4.24).

13. All children's homes should be regularly and formally inspected by local authority inspection units, operating under guidance from the Department of Health and monitored by the Social Services Inspectorate.

Recommendations

13.1 Secretary of State issue a direction to secure the inspection of local authority, controlled and assisted community homes by local authority inspection units (paragraph 4.41).

13.2 Department of Health cause section 60 of the Act to be amended to provide for voluntary homes to be registered and inspected by local authorities (paragraph 4.41).

13.3 Department of Health include in its forthcoming guidance to inspection units on inspecting children's services guidance on the staffing of units and the membership of Advisory Committees; and monitor their performance through the Social Services Inspectorate (paragraph 4.44).

14. Secure accommodation should continue to be approved by the Secretary of State and inspected by the Social Services Inspectorate.

Recommendations

14.1 Secure accommodation in all settings, not already approved by the Secretary of State, become subject to approval by the Secretary of State (paragraph 4.51).

14.2 Government check that the regulatory procedures affecting children in residential placements other than in children's homes are suitable, and imply the same standards of protection where that would be justified (paragraph 4.57).

RESOURCES (CHAPTER 5)

15. The experience of the review confirms that social work is the core discipline of residential child care. Personal care and management are equally important.

16. All heads of homes and a proportion of care staff, possibly amounting to one third in all, should hold the Diploma in Social Work or a relevant professional equivalent. The remainder should possess the appropriate level of the National Vocational Qualification.

Recommendations

16.1 Department of Health and the Local Authority Associations consider what statistical information about the qualifications held by the social services workforce should in future be collected (paragraph 5.7).

16.2 Local authorities plan to secure all officers in charge are qualified to DipSW within 3 years (paragraph 5.12).

16.3 The Joint Inquiry consider the balance of qualification required between DipSW and NVQ among care staff (paragraph 5.13).

16.4 Managers set for unqualified staff clear objectives for personal development, for attainment within specific timetables (paragraph 5.14).

16.5 Department of Health/CCETSW and the Local Authority Associations formulate an action plan within the strategy for social services training to obtain, within 5 years, the output from qualifying training to provide the numbers of qualified staff needed (paragraph 5.17).

16.6 Department of Health/CCETSW and the Local Authority Associations establish an expert group to report within 6 months on the residential child care content of qualifying courses (paragraph 5.17).

16.7 Department of Health give priority to residential care in the first review of the adequacy of child care training under Section 83 of the Act (paragraph 5.18).

16.8 Department of Health re-emphasise the priority for residential child care staff under the 1992-93 Training Support Programme (paragraph 5.18).

17. Salaries should reflect qualifications, performance and experience as well as the nature of the work. Conditions of service should reflect the particular requirements of residential child care.

Recommendation

17.1 The Joint Inquiry consider the review's comments on pay and conditions of service (paragraphs 5.25 and 5.26).

18. Above all, employers need to improve the standing of residential child care as an occupation. The professional associations have a part to play in this.

Recommendation

18.1 Employers and the Joint Inquiry address the issue of raising the status of, and morale among, staff in residential care (paragraph 5.24).

19. Authorities should develop systems for the personnel management and career development of residential child care staff. A managerially-led staffing policy is needed throughout children's services.

Recommendation

19.2 Local Authority Associations/Local Government Management Board draw up guidance on staffing policy, personnel management and career development within 6 months (paragraph 5.23).

20. The design and attractiveness of buildings, and the size of home, are factors affecting quality of care.

21. It is reasonable for unit costs to have gone up faster in residential child care than in other local authority residential services.

Recommendation

21.1 <u>Local and Central Government address constructively the resource implications of the recommendations in this Report through the normal processes (paragraph 5.40).</u>

THE FUTURE (CHAPTER 6)

22. Volume 4 of the Children Act Guidance and Regulations, Residential Care, is impressive in its depth and coverage. It covers most of the subjects considered in this review. Its implementation will materially assist both the care and the protection of children in residential homes.

Recommendations

22.1 <u>Secretary of State consider making periodic public reports of progress in implementing the Children Act (paragraph 6.3).</u>

22.2 <u>Department of Health report in 18 months' time to the Secretary of State on the first year's operation of the Regulations and Guidance, and institute further monitoring if desirable (paragraph 6.4).</u>

APPENDIX 1

**EXTRACT FROM : THE INTRODUCTION TO CHAPTER 1
OF THE CHILDREN ACT 1989
GUIDANCE AND REGULATIONS, VOLUME 4**

1.1   The regulations and guidance in this volume are concerned with the care of children in residential homes of various kinds. They supersede previous regulations and guidance issued some 20 years ago and the opportunity has been taken to adopt a radically new approach to what is needed based on the principles of the Children Act 1989 and the changing tasks of homes. Residential care is a positive and desirable way of providing stability and care for some children which they themselves often prefer to other kinds of placement. Homes should set out to treat each child as an individual person and to promote and safeguard his welfare in every way. In part this will be achieved by planning and review of each child's case as required by the guidance and regulations covering Arrangement of Placements and Review included in later chapters. But homes themselves must exercise the concern that a good parent would by providing a safe environment which promotes the child's development and protects him from exposure to harm in his contacts with other people or experiences in the community. Responsible authorities need to be continually aware of practice in each home and how it contributes to the children's well-being. They should define the principles upon which each home operates and establish standards for practice. The operation of the home must be regularly and carefully monitored. Local authorities and other organisations responsible for several homes should have effective management structures which guide, support, monitor and control all aspects of their work.

1.2   Residential care remains a vital resource, but it is essential to see it as part of the overall network of services for children, used in a planned way and when it is in the best interests of the individual child. The major principles underlying the Children Act about partnership with parents, involvement of children and those with parental responsibility in decision making, proper planning and review, the right to make representations and so on, apply equally to children in residential settings and should help to ensure that their placement there is not seen in isolation from overall services to provide support to families and to children in need.

1.3   The way in which children's homes are used in the care of children has changed greatly in recent years. Whilst residential solutions are used less frequently overall, the young people in the homes are older than before, and older than other young people in care. Placements are frequently of short duration and some are made at critical times when other arrangements are changing or have broken down. Changes elsewhere in the care system, such as the efforts to reduce the use of custody for young offenders, may also have an effect on the use of children's homes. Children's homes are provided for a range of purposes: some are a long-term base for a child growing up; others provide accommodation for a period while specific tasks are achieved. Some of the children have suffered the most distressing life experiences and working with them calls for skills of the highest order.

1.4   The Act and Regulations, as well as the guidance, make significant demands on those responsible for children's homes and it is hoped that the new legislative provisions will help bring about important improvements in the level of service provided in homes. This guidance describes the basic requirements for providing good child care in general, but different aspects of the provision will require different emphasis depending on the nature of each home and the needs of the children.

1.5   The Regulations and Guidance are designed to provide a framework of practice for the running of children's homes which emphasises the importance of safeguarding and promoting the welfare of individual children. They are not intended to be a detailed guide to good practice. The National Institute of Social Work (NISW) has been commissioned to produce with the Wagner Development Group further guidance on residential services for children and young people, along the lines of "Home Life - a Code of Practice for Residential Care" (published by the Centre for Policy on Ageing in 1984) which deals with adult residential care. This is expected to be available in 1992.

1.6 Although the administrative arrangements for the different kinds of homes governed by the Regulations are different, the aim is that the requirements with regard to the welfare of each child in the home and the conduct of the home should be subject to the same standards of provision and child care practices.

1.7 Good practice encompasses both the running of the home and individual care and planning for each child. There is a need to be particularly sensitive to some issues in group care. Children being looked after will have very different family backgrounds and different needs and will be subject to individual child care plans. Homes must be run so as to be able to respond to each child as an individual. Whilst there is a need for each child to conform to shared "house rules" which foster mutual respect within group living, the institutional needs of the Home should never be allowed to dominate the lives of children and staff. Safeguarding the child's personal possessions and encouraging the child to develop ownership of some part of their surroundings is extremely important.

1.8 The concept of partnership between parents, children, Local Authorities and voluntary organisations is central to the Act and Regulations. Particular guidance is given in Chapter 4 - Contact.

APPENDIX 2

LIST OF WITNESSES
WHO GAVE ORAL EVIDENCE TO THE REVIEW

Mrs Barbara Kahan O.B.E., M.A.		
Mr Allan Levy Q.C., LL.B		
Mr Richard Clough M.B.E.,	General Secretary	Social Care Association (SCA)
Mr Stephen Campbell,	Under Secretary,	Association of County Councils ACC)
Mr Peter Westland,	Under Secretary,	Association of Metropolitan Authorities (AMA)
Mr Paul Marwood		Local Government Management Board (LGMB)
Ms Mary Moss		National Association for Young Persons in Care (NAYPIC)
Ms Rachel Hodgkin		The Children's Legal Centre
Mr David Jones,	General Secretary,	British Association of Social Workers (BASW)
Mr Christopher Andrews		British Association of Social Workers (BASW)
Mr John Ransford,	Director,	(ADSS) North Yorkshire Social Services Department
Mr Peter Smallridge,	Director,	(ADSS) Warwickshire Social Services Department
Mr Ian White,	Director,	(ADSS) Oxfordshire Social Services Department
Mr Tony Hall,	Director,	Central Council for Education and Training in Social Work (CCETSW)
Mr Peter Fry,	Social Work Education Adviser,	Central Council for Education and Training in Social Work (CCETSW)
Mr Eddie Conneely		Residential Child Care Worker, London
Mr Dudley St. Aubyn Roach		Residential Child Care Worker, Berkshire
Mr Stephen Eyre		Residential Child Care Worker, Warwickshire
Mr Robin Whistlecraft		Residential Child Care Worker, Coventry
Mr Tom White,	Director,	National Children's Home (NCH)
Mr J Findlay,	Assistant National Officer,	National Association of Local Government Officers (NALGO)
Mr George Thomas,	Director,	Child Care (NCVCCO)
Mr Roger Singleton,	Senior Director,	Barnardo's
Ms Judith King		Dartmouth House Residential Home
Ms Gwen James		Voice for the Child in Care
Mr Terry Connor,	Director (London Region),	The Catholic Children's Society

APPENDIX 3

LIST OF WRITTEN REPRESENTATIONS

Captain N C Baird-Murray	Director	Shaftesbury Homes and Arethusa
Ms M Belville	Lay Visitor	Lewisham
David Berridge	Research Development Director	National Children's Bureau
Ms J Berry	Senior Lecturer in Applied Social Administration (Retired)	University of Sheffield
Malcolm Billinge	Senior Educational Psychologist	Devon County Council
Lord Brabourne	Chairman	Council of Caldecott Community
Roger Bullock		Dartington Social Research Unit, University of Bristol
Dr Alison Campbell		Campbell & Devore Associates Ltd., Social & Market Research
Keith Drinkwater	Regional Director (London & South East)	The Children's Society
Teddy Gold	Consultant	Priority Area Development, Neighbourhood Council & Community Development Consultants, Liverpool
Harriet Harman MP		
Mr Denis Harvey	Principal	Hillside School, Fife
Mr Maurice Hawker	Director of Social Services	Essex County Council
Ms Gina Hawkins		Community Tutor & Foster Parent, Rotherham
Hill End Adolescent Unit		Hill End Hospital, Hertfordshire
Mr J Hopkins	Department of Applied Social Studies and Social Work	University of Keele
Valerie Howarth	Executive Director	Childline
Tory Laughland	Editor	Who Cares? Magazine
Cllr S Marks	Chair	Inner London Juvenile Liaison Committee
Mrs P Mundy	Director	Five Rivers Residential Project, Salisbury
Mr Peter Newell	Co-ordinator	End Physical Punishment Of Children
Phillip Noyes	Director of Public Policy	The National Society for the Prevention of Cruelty to Children
John Ogden	Principal Adviser	London Boroughs Children's Regional Planning Committee
Granville Orange	Professional Officer	The Children's Family Trust
Chris Payne	Consultant in Social Care	National Institute for Social Work
Professor Colin Pritchard	Professor of Social Work Studies	University of Southampton
Dennis Quickfall		Residential Care Worker
Mr Simon Randall	Chairman	London Boroughs Association Housing & Social Services Committee
Mr J M Richards	Director	The Catholic Children's Society (Westminster)
Mr A L Smart		Former Assistant Officer in Charge (Child Care), Leicestershire
Professor G Upton and others	School of Education	University of Birmingham
Adrian Ward	Lecturer in Social Work	University of Reading
Dr Margaret White JP		Former Assistant Medical Officer for Health
Caroline Whitehead	Associate Director (Development)	The Peper Harow Foundation
Mrs M Wilkes		Former Teacher and Residential Care Worker

APPENDIX 4

BIBLIOGRAPHY

Part 1: List of publications which are mentioned in the text of the Report

1. BEBBINGTON A. and MILES J. (1989): *"The Background of Children who enter Local Authority Care"*. British Journal of Social Work, (1989), 19: 349-368.

2. PARKER R. and MILLHAM S. (1989): *"Introduction: Research on Organisation and Accountability for State Intervention"*. in HUDSON J. and GALAWAY B. (eds.): *"The State as Parent"*. NATO ASI series D, Vol 53, 1989.

3. SOCIAL SERVICES INSPECTORATE (1985): *"Inspection of Community Homes, September 1985"*. SSI, Department of Health and Social Security, London.

4. DEPARTMENT OF HEALTH (1990): *"The Care of Children: Principles and Practice in Regulations and Guidance"*. Consultant - Jane Rowe, HMSO, London.

5. AUDIT INSPECTORATE (1981): *"The Provision of Child Care: A Study of Eight Local Authorities in England and Wales"*. Department of the Environment.

6. AUDIT COMMISSION (1985): *"Child Care Report"*.

7. ROWE J. HUNDLEBY M. and GARNETT L. (1989): *"Child Care Now"*. BAFF, Research Series 6.

8. BERRIDGE D. (1985): *"Children's Homes"*. Basil Blackwell.

9. BERRIDGE D. (1991): *"Personal Communication to the Review"*.

10. DEPARTMENT OF HEALTH (1991): *"Patterns and Outcomes in Child Placement"*. Consultant - Jane Rowe, HMSO, London.

11. BARN R. (1990): *"Black Children in Local Authority Care: Admission Patterns"*. New Community, 16(2): 229-236.

12. LONDON BOROUGHS CHILDREN'S REGIONAL PLANNING COMMITTEE (1989): *"Equal Opportunities"*. Report of a Working Party, January 1989.

13. PARKER R. (1988): *"Residential Care for Children"*. in SINCLAIR I (ed.): *"Residential Care: The Research Reviewed"*. HMSO, London.

14. SOCIAL SERVICES INSPECTORATE (1989): *"Review of Residential Services for Children in Care: Richmond"*. SSI London Region,

Department of Health.

15. WAGNER G. (1988): *"Residential Care: A Positive Choice"*. HMSO, London.

16. LONDON BOROUGHS CHILDREN'S REGIONAL PLANNING COMMITTEE (1991): *"A Strategy for Residential Child Care in London 1991-2000"*. Consultation Paper, LBCRPC, July 1991.

17. DEPARTMENT OF HEALTH AND SOCIAL SECURITY (1988): *"Working Together"*: A guide to arrangements for inter-agency co-operation for the protection of children from abuse. HMSO London.

18. JACKSON S. 1988 *"The Education of Children in Care"* Bristol Papers No 1, Univ of Bristol, School of Applied Social Services.

19. STEIN M. and CAREY K. (1986): *"Leaving Care"*. Basil Blackwell.

20. SOCIAL SERVICES INSPECTORATE (1990): *"Child Care Policy: Putting it in Writing"*. Diana Robbins, Department of Health (SSI) HMSO, London.

21. STEIN M. (1989): *"Leaving Care"*. in KAHAN B. (ed.): *"Child Care Research. Policy and Practice"*. Hodder and Stoughton in association with the Open University.

22. DEPARTMENT OF HEALTH AND SOCIAL SECURITY (1981): *"Control and Discipline in Community Homes"*. Report of a Working Party.

23. DEPARTMENT OF HEALTH AND SOCIAL SECURITY (1988): *"Violence to Staff"*.

24. DE'ATH E. (1989): *"Families and Children"*. in KAHAN B. (ed.): *"Child Care Research. Policy and Practice"*. Hodder and Stoughton in association with the Open University.

25. NEWMAN C. (1989): *"Young Runaways: Findings from Britain's First Safe House"*. Children's Society, London.

26. BERRY J. (1975): *"Daily Experience of Residential Life"*. Routledge and Kegan Paul.

27. BERRY J. (1989): *"Daily Experience in Residential Care for Children and their Caregivers"*. in MORGAN S. and RIGHTON P. (eds.): *"Child Care: Concerns and Conflicts"*. Hodder and Stoughton in association with the Open University.

28. SOCIAL SERVICES INSPECTORATE (1991): *"Inspecting for Quality"*. HMSO, London.

29. DEPARTMENT OF HEALTH AND SOCIAL SECURITY (1985): *"Social Work Decisions in Child Care"*. (Pink Book) Consultant - Jane Rowe, HMSO, London.

30. MILLHAM ET AL. (1989): *"Access Disputes in Child Care"*. Gower.

31. DEPARTMENT OF HEALTH (1991): *"Implementing Community Care: Purchaser, Commissioner and Provider Roles"*. HMSO, London.

32. LONDON BOROUGH OF BRENT (1985): *"A Child in Trust"*.

33. UNIVERSITY OF LEICESTER (1990): *"Children in Need and their Families - A Guide for Local Authority Councillors to Part III of the Children Act, 1989"*. School of Social Work, University of Leicester.

34. KNAPP M AND SMITH J (1985): *"The Costs of Residential Child Care: Explaining Variations in the Public Sector"*. Policy and Politics, Vol 13, No 2.

Part 2: List of publications which are not mentioned in the Report but which informed the views reflected in it

ADCOCK M. WHITE R. and ROWLANDS O. (1988): *"The Administrative Parent"*. British Agencies for Adoption and Fostering.

AHMAD B. (1990): *"Black Perspectives in Social Work"*. Venture Press in association with the National Institute of Social Work.

BEEDELL C. (1970): *"Residential Life with Children"*. Routledge and Kegan Paul.

COLTON M. (1986): *"Dimensions of Substitute Care"*. D. Phil. Oxford.

COLTON M. (1988): *"Substitute Care Practice"*. Adoption and Fostering, Vol.12, No.1.

CURTIS COMMITTEE (1946): *"Report of the Care of Children Committee"*. Cmd. 6922.

GOFFMAN E. (1968): *"Asylums"*. Pelican Books.

GRIFFITHS R. SIR (1988): *"Community Care: Agenda for Action"*. HMSO, London.

HARDING L. (1989): *"Two Value Positions in Recent Child Care Law and Practice"*. in MORGAN S. and RIGHTON P. (eds.): *"Child Care: Concerns and Conflicts"*. Hodder and Stoughton in association with the Open University.

HOLMAN R. (1980): *"A Real Child Care Policy for the Future"*. Community Care, No.340, pp. 16-17.

MILLHAM S. BULLOCK R. HOSIE K. and HAAK M. (1986): *"Lost in Care: The Problem of Maintaining Links Between Children in Care and Their Families"*. Gower.

PACKMAN J. (1968): *"Child Care: Needs and Numbers"*. Allen and Unwin, London.

International Research Perspectives on Interventions with Young Persons". NATO ASI Series, Series D, Vol. 53. Kluwer Academic Publishers.

PARKER R. (1989): *"Theme and Variations"*. in KAHAN B. (ed.): *"Child Care Research, Policy and Practice"*. Hodder and Stoughton in association with the Open University.

RAYNOR P. (1985): *"Social Work. Justice and Control"*. Basil Blackwell.

ROWE J. and LAMBERT L. (1973): *"Children who Wait"*. Association of British Adoption Agencies.

SOCIAL SERVICES INSPECTORATE (1989): *"The Residential Care of Children, Birmingham Social Services Department"*. SSI West Midlands Region, Department of Health.

SOCIAL SERVICES INSPECTORATE (1988): *"Residential Care in Knowsley"*. SSI, Department of Health.

SOCIAL SERVICES INSPECTORATE (1991): *"Review of Residential Child Care Services in Southwark, March 1991"*. SSI London Region, Department of Health.

WATERHOUSE L. (1989): *"In Defence of Residential Care"*. in MORGAN S. and RIGHTON P. (eds.): *"Child Care: Concerns and Conflicts"*. Hodder and Stoughton in association with the Open University.

APPENDIX 5

LOCAL AUTHORITY FINANCE:
HOW THE SYSTEM WORKS

Sources of Finance

1. Local authorities have two main sources of money:
    - money given out by the Government
    - money from the community charge

    The money given out by the Government comes partly in the form of grants funded from general taxation and partly from businesses which pay rates at a level set by central Government. Together the money given out by the Government is known as Aggregate External Finance (AEF).

2. Business rates differ from the old system of rates because:
    - the Government (not the local authority) now decides what the rate will be, and it is the same throughout the country; and
    - the money is collected by local authorities and passed on to the Treasury.

3. The level of AEF for any year is fixed. If the income from business rates is higher than planned, the Treasury keeps the surplus and pays it out the following year, so reducing the contribution from general taxation. If the income were to be lower, the Treasury would have to find the extra money.

4. Local authorities also have other sources of income:
    - they can charge for some services
    - they can obtain income from the sale of property
    - they can borrow money to fund capital projects.

5. The Government exercises some control over all these sources of income:
    - Local authorities' powers to charge (in some cases their duty to charge) are laid down by legislation
    - a proportion (generally half) of income from sale of property must go towards reducing local authorities' debts, if any
    - Local authorities can borrow money only to the extent that they are permitted to do so by the credit approvals issued by the Government (see below).

6. There is one other important difference between local authority budgets and central Government budgets. Local authorities are allowed to have reserves - that is to say they can raise money one year for spending in another year.

7. For the most part, local authorities can spend whatever money they have on whatever they like (provided it is within their powers laid down by Parliament). In the jargon, the money is unhypothecated.

Standard Spending

8. Standard spending is the amount the Government thinks is sufficient to provide a standard level of service with standard efficiency. There are three main levels:
    - Total Standard Spending (TSS) - the total amount the Government thinks local authorities should spend;
    - "service block" totals - the amounts the Government thinks local authorities, as a group, should be spending on particular services such as education or social services;
    - Standard Spending Assessments (SSAs) - the amounts the Government thinks each individual local authority should spend.

The Local Authority Settlement

9. The Government decides what TSS and AEF should be after a Cabinet Committee has considered the views of the Local Authority Associations and Government Departments on what they consider local authorities will need to spend in the following year, in the light of what the Government believes it can afford to contribute. The outcome of Ministerial consideration is announced by the Secretary of State for the Environment in the local authority settlement statement in July.

The Service Split

10. A decision is also needed on how TSS should be divided between the service blocks because it affects the distribution of TSS - and hence AEF - between authorities.

How TSS is distributed between authorities

11. Each local authority has a Standard Spending Assessment (SSA), which represents the amount the Government thinks that authority should spend. The SSA is built up from SSAs for the individual services for which that authority is responsible. Not all authorities are responsible for all types of service (the most notable split being between shire counties and shire districts) but, in all, there are 12 service SSAs - 5 for education, 3 for personal social services (PSS), and one each for the policy, fire and civil defence, highway maintenance and other services (There is a thirteenth SSA, for capital financing: see paragraph 17 below). Each SSA is based on formulae which take account of particular characteristics of each authority which have been found to be relevant following extensive analysis, research and discussion with local authority representatives. The SSA formulae are kept under review.

12. The three PSS SSAs cover services for children, services for the elderly, and services for other adults. The children's services SSA takes account of the number of children "at risk" in each area, and the additional cost of providing care for children from poor social conditions. The SSA for services for elderly people takes account of the numbers of elderly people likely to need residential or domiciliary services. The SSA for services for other adults takes account of social conditions. All three SSAs take account of the differences in costs in different parts of the country.

13. It is important to remember that SSAs simply share out the totals for services which have already been agreed by Ministers - changing the formulae inevitably means that some authorities gain, whilst others lose.

14. The Secretary of State for the Environment consults the Local Authority Associations and his Ministerial colleagues on any changes to the SSA formulae he wishes to propose and publishes draft SSAs in October. Local authorities then have a chance to comment and Parliament debates the proposals. Final SSAs are published in January.

Local Authority Finance and PES

15. The local authority settlement process runs parallel with, and to a rather earlier timetable than, the Public Expenditure Survey (PES) process. The bulk of Government support to local authorities is carried on the Department of Environment Vote. But three elements of local authority finance do find their way into Department of Health's PES process, namely:

- specific grants
- capital grants
- credit approvals.

16. Specific grants and capital grants are given to local authorities for specific purposes and have to be bid for in PES, though specific grants come out of the PSS service share of TSS. They enable money to be targeted at Ministerial priorities (almost invariably specific grants are only paid if local authorities make a contribution to the cost of whatever it is that is being supported by the grant).

17. Credit approvals represent the amount a local authority is allowed to borrow to finance capital expenditure. Borrowing money costs money (hence the inclusion of a SSA for capital financing) and capital expenditure often has revenue consequences - two good reasons for controlling credit approvals through PES.

18. It is important to note that local authorities have other ways of financing capital spending - notably receipts from sales, or from revenue expenditure derived as above. So an assessment has to be made of the likely total need for capital spending on social services and of how much can be paid for from other sources before a bid for credit approvals can be decided upon.

19. Most credit approvals are unhypothecated, so even if the Department of Health obtains a certain level of credit approvals in PES there is no guarantee that they will be used for social services projects.

20. The remaining credit approvals which Department of Health wins in PES are added to a figure for Receipts Taken Into Account (RTIAs) (agreed inter-Departmentally in advance of the PES bids) which recognises that local authorities can use receipts to help finance capital spending. The total figure is the Annual Capital Guidelines (ACGs) and these are distributed to local authorities. For the social services the method of distribution is decided by Department of Health Ministers after consulting the Local Authority Associations. Currently a weighted population formula is used which gives more money to local authorities with large numbers of very elderly people. A similar process is gone through by other Departments. The Department of the Environment then add up all the ACGs issued by the Various Departments to a particular local authority, deduct an amount for RTIAs (which Department of the Environment decide) and issue the balance as unhypothecated credit approvals.

21. Ministers may, with the agreement of Treasury, target credit approvals at specific services. Where this happens the credit approvals become supplementary credit approvals (SCAs). In social services, SCAs, were issued in 1991/92 for services for the mentally ill, AIDS and HIV patients and for information technology which local authorities need in connection with the community care reforms.

Charge Capping

22. Local authorities are required to draw up a budget and send it to the Department of the Environment in March. If, in the Secretary of State for the Environment's view, an authority's budget is excessive or shows an excessive increase over the previous year's budget, that authority's budget can be capped, either to the level of their SSA or some level above it. The Department of Health has the chance to make representations about the possible effects of capping on the social services provided by any authority which is faced with capping, both when the caps are set and again if authorities appeal against the level of the cap. In 1990 the Secretary of State for the Environment told authorities in October how he expected to decide whether a 1991-92 budget or budget increase was excessive, and has announced his intention to do so for 1992-93.

APPENDIX 6

SURVEY OF CARE STAFF IN MAINTAINED AND CONTROLLED COMMUNITY HOMES : QUALIFICATIONS AND LENGTH OF TIME IN POST

Methodology

1. A sample of twenty local authorities were asked to complete a questionnaire covering qualifications and the length of service in their current post. The questionnaires needed to be returned in two weeks. The number of staff employed in community homes varies considerably between authorities, and a fairly small proportion of authorities account for a sizeable element of the workforce. (At 30 September 1990 about 50 per cent of the workforce were employed by just 24 authorities.) The sample was designed to ensure good coverage of the larger authorities. The sample was chosen randomly within size groups; authorities who employed no staff directly were not included in the survey. The survey of twenty authorities is estimated to represent about a quarter of the total workforce.

2. The sample design does mean that the results of the survey need to be weighted to represent the England distribution of large and small authorities. The results reported in the main body of the report are so adjusted.

Coverage

3. The questionnaire asked the authorities to divide the workforce into officers in charge (the person in sole charge of a home), assistant officers in charge (staff with some but not the sole management responsibility) and other care staff. The other dimension covered was length of time in current post.

Response

4. All authorities were able to make full returns. One authority made a separate entry for children's centres that had both residential and non residential functions.

Findings

5. These are set out in the main body of the report in global terms. It should be emphasized that the overall results are the results of a sample of about twenty authorities (one fifth of the authorities in England). The results should not be regarded as a definitive statement of the England position. The England percentages could be rather larger or smaller than the estimates.

6. This is true of all sample surveys but there was a good deal of variation between the individual authorities (varying for example between two thirds of all the officers in charge having CQSW in one authority to none in another: both authorities had about twenty officers in charge and were in adjacent areas). The level of qualified staff depends on the individual policies of authorities; so the results of the survey are particularly dependent on the choice of sample, and lead to some difficulties in predicting likely England levels, especially among officers in charge where the numbers are much smaller. There were variations in the other staff groups, too, particularly to the extent that these staff had care qualifications other than CQSW. The percentage of "other care staff" with some qualification varied from 0 per cent to 60 per cent. However the proportion of staff in the assistant officer and other care staff group having CQSW showed much less variation and could be regarded as being a good indicator of England levels.

WEIGHTED SURVEY RESULTS

PERCENTAGE OF OFFICERS IN CHARGE
BY SERVICE IN CURRENT POST AND QUALIFICATIONS

	LESS THAN 6 MTHS	6 MTHS BUT < 2YRS	2 OR MORE YEARS	TOTAL
CQSW	3.85%	10.79%	16.18%	30.82%
CSS	3.51%	8.84%	30.25%	42.59%
OTHER 1.01%	1.63%	4.36%	7.00%	
NONE OF THESE	1.15%	2.88%	15.56%	19.59%
TOTAL	9.52%	24.14%	66.35%	100.00%

PERCENTAGE OF ASSISTANT OFFICERS IN CHARGE
BY SERVICES IN CURRENT POST AND QUALIFICATIONS

	LESS THAN 6 MTHS	6 MTHS BUT < 2YRS	2 OR MORE YEARS	TOTAL
CQSW	0.42%	2.01%	4.38%	6.81%
CSS	2.27%	3.02%	15.92%	21.22%
OTHER	0.44%	5.12%	10.22%	15.77%
NONE OF THESE	4.35%	19.23%	32.63%	56.20%
TOTAL	7.48%	29.38%	63.15%	100.00%

PERCENTAGE OF OTHER CARE STAFF BY SERVICE
IN CURRENT POST AND QUALIFICATIONS

	LESS THAN 6 MTHS	6 MTHS BUT < 2YRS	2 OR MORE YEARS	TOTAL
CQSW	0.08%	0.18%	0.52%	0.78%
CSS	0.47%	0.75%	3.18%	4.40%
OTHER	1.06%	2.76%	12.81%	16.64%
NONE OF THESE	9.64%	30.57%	37.98%	78.19%
TOTAL	11.25%	34.27%	54.48%	100.00%

TOTAL CARE STAFF BY SERVICE IN POST AND QUALIFICATIONS

	LESS THAN 6 MTHS	6 MTHS BUT < 2YRS	2 OR MORE YEARS	TOTAL
CQSW	0.4%	1.3%	2.4%	4.2%
CSS	1.0%	1.8%	7.6%	10.4%
OTHER	0.9%	3.1%	11.7%	15.7%
NONE OF THESE	8.0%	26.3%	35.3%	69.6%
TOTAL	10.4%	32.6%	57.0%	100.0%

Printed in the United Kingdom for HMSO
Dd 295219 C00